All God's People

All God's People
working with all ages

edited by Leslie J Francis
and
Anne Faulkner

Gracewing.

First published in 1997

Gracewing
Fowler Wright Books
2 Southern Avenue, Leominster
Herefordshire HR6 0QF

ISBN 0 85244 356 0

Typesetting by Action Typesetting Ltd,
Gloucester, GL1 1SP

Printed by Cromwell Press
Broughton Gifford, Wiltshire SN12 8PH

CONTENTS

Preface   vi

Introduction   vii

1   Candlemas   *Michael Sturdy*   1

2   Stations of the cross   *Anne Thorne*   14

3   Way of the cross   *Stephen Cottrell*   21

4   Deanery Pentecost   *Anne Faulkner*   31

5   Teddy's Pentecost   *Betty Pedley*   43

6   Carnival time   *Anne Faulkner*   53

7   Involving schools   *Martin Warner*   64

8   Saint James   *Brian R Tubbs*   74

9   Walking the way   *Stephen Cottrell*   80

10 Splash out   *Betty Pedley*   88

11 Saint Mary   *Angela Warwick*   96

12 New beginnings   *Anne Faulkner*   103

13 Team spirit   *Anne Faulkner*   116

14 Saints alive   *Margaret Dean*   132

15 Fire! Fire!   *Gill Ambrose*   140

Appendices

1   Children and the law   *Marion Richards*   154

2   Family services   *Leslie J Francis*   166

Contributors   175

Preface

This book is about good practice in the local church. It celebrates the imagination, creativity and commitment of clergy and lay people concerned with learning and worship among all ages of God's people. We wish to make these examples of good practice more widely known to encourage other churches to develop their own ministries.

Our job as editors has been to witness what others have been doing and to encourage them to tell their tale. We are grateful both to those friends and colleagues who have contributed chapters and to the many more who have stimulated our thinking and confirmed our confidence in the vitality and strength which exists in the local church.

Our special thanks go also to those who have worked with us in shaping this book: to Diane Drayson for coordinating the diverse contributions and bringing them into a coherent style; to Anne Rees for preparing the manuscript; to Susan Jones and Peter Faulkner for commenting on draft text.

Leslie J Francis
Anne Faulkner

January 1997

Introduction

Research projects, working parties and church reports can all help to stimulate and encourage the church's primary work of mission and nurture. It is the clergy and laity in the parishes and in the dioceses, however, who put this work into practice. In this book the voices of these local people are heard.

Each chapter concentrates on one specific example illustrating how a local church, or a group of local churches, or even a whole diocese, has set out to work imaginatively and creatively with God's people of all ages.

Each local tale, however, has been told according to the same clear pattern and to provide answers to the same fundamental questions: why, who, where, when and how. In this way the reader is able quite quickly to build up a clear picture of each project.

Every church is different and every local situation is unique. It is a mistake, therefore, to imagine that what has worked well in one place can be transplanted directly to another place. By illustrating a variety of different practices in a variety of different places, this book hopes to stimulate and to encourage other churches to experiment and to share what they learn with the wider church.

Since each chapter deals with one specific example, the chapters can be read in any order. In the book the chapters are simply ordered according to the progression of the secular and sacred calendars, starting with Candlemas in February and culminating with bonfire night in November. Some intervening chapters explore themes from the church's calendar, like Lent, Good Friday, Pentecost and the feast of All Saints. Other intervening chapters explore important points in the secular calendar, like the local carnival, the Summer school holiday and the beginning of the new school year.

The appendices focus on two key issues which underpin many of the chapters. The first issue concerns the Children Act 1989 and the legal implications of this act for the ways in which churches undertake their work among young people.

The second issue concerns that form of worship which is often known as family services.

The autonomy of the individual chapters should make the book particularly helpful for parish discussion groups and working groups. For example, if a local church is considering planning an event for Pentecost, chapters four or five could provide a good starting point. Similarly, local churches may wish to focus on the specific issues raised in the appendices regarding the implications of the Children Act 1989 or family services.

While this book begins with the specific experiences of the various authors within their own context, its future now lies very much in the hands of the readers. Its potential will only be fulfilled if it succeeds in inspiring in new places proper experimentation and good practice in the church's work among *All God's People.*

1 CANDLEMAS

Michael Sturdy

Why

Wokingham is a former market town that now has a large commuter population. The parish of All Saints includes the town centre, some of the older estates and one of the newest. The congregation is very mixed but includes quite a high proportion of professional people.

A fairly recent minute of the education committee at the church of All Saints in the town of Wokingham reads:

> The Advent workshop was so well received, we should have a follow up.

In a previous year, the congregation had organised a workshop for Advent and this had left them wanting more. Candlemas suggested itself for the next effort because it allowed time for planning, it was not too far away, and it was intriguing because it was not a festival that was high in the awareness of the congregation. Not very many people knew much about it. The theme chosen was 'The light of the world'.

The plan was to arrange a day workshop that would be educational, would be enjoyable in itself, and would result in a contribution to worship at the 9.30 service on the following Sunday morning.

Who

The workshop was to be open to members of the congregation, including the uniformed organisations. As the 9.30 service on the chosen Sunday was a parade service, the uniformed organisations would normally be present.

It was decided at the outset that the workshop should be for all ages, with provision for a crèche if requested, so that no-one should feel unable to come.

Where

The workshop was held in the Church of England junior school in the parish. This has areas for individual group work and is more spacious and suitable than the church annexe, which does not have many rooms.

When

The idea of a workshop was first put forward in July at a meeting of All Saints education committee. At the next meeting of this committee in the following September, a small steering group was formed to take over the detailed planning. The workshop itself was held on Saturday, 1st February, and was linked to the 9.30 parish communion the next day.

The decision to hold the workshop on the Saturday, the day before Candlemas, pre-empted any question of whether the parish should celebrate the actual day or the nearest Sunday.

How: planning

At the first planning meeting the organiser of the Advent workshop was invited to reflect on the strengths and weaknesses of the event, so that lessons could be learnt and good ideas used again. Thereafter detailed planning was done by two members of the education committee, who formed a subcommittee and reported back regularly, but were otherwise autonomous. Useful suggestions came from the full committee, whose members also volunteered to fill gaps if necessary. The venue was booked as early in proceedings as possible.

A list of possible activity sessions was drawn up, together with the names of people who might lead each one. This proved not too difficult, although one or two ideas had to be dropped, and two of the leaders were only found after the first leaders' meeting. Minimum ages were set for some activities: 9 or 10 years old for liturgical dance, 4 years old for baking, 12 years old for church decoration unless accompanied by an adult, 6 years old for candle making unless accompanied by an adult.

Two preparation sessions were held for leaders of the workshop, one in December and one in January. At the first leaders' meeting some background material on Candlemas from *The Promise of His Glory* and *Welcoming the Light of Christ* was presented, together with an outline programme. There was a lot of detailed discussion about issues like materials, requirements and restrictions. This meeting also suggested hymns for the Sunday service. Apart from this, leaders were left very much to work out their own session format.

The aim of the second leaders' meeting was to confirm details and boost confidence. It also gave a chance for the new leaders to meet the rest of the team.

Agreement with the clergy was reached about the form of the service on the Sunday, which was to be based on liturgy in *The Promise of His Glory* with contributions from the previous day's activities. At first it was thought that the difficulty of predicting what would result from the activity sessions would make it impossible to have a fixed order of service, but it was decided to write a framework with slots that might or might not be filled from the activities. The planning subcommittee was given a free hand to do this and in the end a printed order of service was prepared.

How: budget

Activity costs varied. One pound was requested for church decorations while a charge of 50p was made for the candle making and banner activities. Donations for refreshments were also requested. Efforts to collect these were not strenuous but some contribution was made to expenses.

How: publicity

The first publicity was an insert in the Sunday notice sheets on the first Sunday in January, which announced the event and invited participants to return booking slips committing themselves to the day and selecting from the available activities. The leaders of all uniformed organisations were contacted individually and asked to tell their groups of the event. They were also given copies of the written publicity. The insert was included in the notice sheets for three successive Sundays, and posters were put up in the porch and the annexe two Sundays before the event.

Some activities were only able to cater for a limited number, and it was hoped to give the leaders some idea of the ages and numbers they could expect. In the event most slips were returned so late that this was not achieved.

How: programme

12.00 – 12.45	Time together – bring your own lunch
12.45 – 1.00	Introduction
1.00 – 2.15	First activity session
2.15 – 2.45	Tea
2.45 – 4.00	Second activity session
4.15 – 5.00	Run through in church
5.00 – 5.15	Service of light

How: events

Informal lunch

The workshop began with a bring-your-own lunch which allowed people to get to know each other and also gave time to sort out changes to the activity allocations.

Introduction

After lunch, everyone met together for a short introduction

and prayer. This introduction included a welcome and an outline of the programme for the day ahead. Activity leaders were presented and the activity venues were explained. After a prayer, the activities began.

Activity sessions

There were nine prepared activities, detailed below. The first two, church choral music and church decoration, were double sessions, that is, participants attended one of these activities for both sessions. This was because the leaders felt that two sessions were needed to do something worthwhile for the 9.30 Sunday service. It was originally planned that the liturgical dance group would also have a double session, but nearly all the participants who chose this activity wanted to do a second activity as well. It was changed to a single session on the understanding that this would not give adequate time to prepare anything that could be performed at the Sunday service.

The remaining activities either had two independent sessions or a single session, depending on demand. Some leaders put a maximum limit on the size of their activity, so these were given two sessions if demand exceeded this. Whether the single sessions were in the first or second period was arranged so that as nearly as possible everyone could go to the sessions of their choice.

The run through in church

After the activity sessions had ended and the clearing up had been done, everyone walked to the church for a run-through of contributions from the activity sessions for the family communion next day. This was led by one of the planning sub-committee, and proved to be a bit chaotic. The idea was first to tell participants roughly what would happen at the service, then to find out from each group what they wanted to contribute and to allow them to practise using the microphone. Although this was very valuable for each group when it was their turn, it meant a lot of waiting about for everyone else and also overran its time.

Service of light

After the run through, the deacon led an informal Service of Light which was taken directly from *The Promise of His Glory*. At the beginning the dancers performed their dance. The candles lit were some of those made by the candle making group.

It was a very moving service, enhanced by the presence of several parents who were not at the workshop but who had arrived early to collect their children.

How: activities

Church choral music

A group of about 8 non-choir members was introduced to church choral music. After a brief outline of its history, the group did some vocal exercises. They began to learn the piece of music 'Arise and shine for your light is come', to be sung as the gradual anthem before the gospel at the 9.30 service the following morning. This music has parts for a small choir as well as for a full choir. The small choir parts were learnt. There was also a refrain for the congregation to sing. During the second activity session, the group went over to the church to practise with the organ before everyone else arrived for the rehearsal.

Church decoration

After an introduction to the theme of Candlemas and an outline of some of the traditions associated with it, this group of six people created a number of flower and foliage arrangements in the shape of yule logs to decorate the church for the next day. For the colour theme of the flowers they took the white of purity, the golden yellow of light, joy and glory, and the violet/purple/blue of penitence and meditation. For foliage they used evergreens which are symbolic of eternal life and hope. Holly represents grief and tribulation, while clinging ivy represents life eternal and fidelity.

Baking

This was attended by between 6 and 8 people who baked rolls. Half of the rolls were used for communion the next day. It is easier to use a bread mix for this kind of bread making as time for proving is very limited.

Candle making

For weeks before the day, people had been encouraged to bring along old candle ends. These were melted down according to colour into shapes that looked a bit like coloured cow pats. These attracted much attention, especially from the children. Every participant had a chance to make a dipped candle, to make a moulded candle and to decorate a bought candle. The group divided into three sub-groups and did each activity in rotation.

For the dipped candles everyone had a piece of wick, which they then dipped alternately in hot wax and cold water until it was fat enough. The moulded candles were made in small plastic tubs (tiny yoghurt size). The length of wick was held in place with a cocktail stick and Blu-tack. Hot wax was poured into the tub and the moulds were left to set. Decoration of candles was done with hot spoons held onto the candles to soften the wax slightly before transfers, dried flowers, or coloured papers were fixed on them. The wax quickly hardens and the decorations remain. To help this process the bought candles were over dipped in white wax in advance.

The process was messy and needed very careful supervision because of the hot wax. Children had help and were not permitted to pour the hot melted wax. The results were very pleasing and were admired.

Banner making

This session requires a wide selection of material. The background material, which is likely to be the only expense, is critical and the leader needs to be careful to bring in a wide selection. Dressmakers in the congregation can be asked to supply remnants for the foreground.

There were about 8 people in this group. The first stage was to read the background material about Candlemas. Then the group brainstormed ideas and images leading to a rough design on paper. At this stage the group decided the banner would not have any words on it. At the bottom would be a crib, above that a cross with flames around it, and at the top a crown. Once the background material was chosen, the group split into sub-groups to design different areas, trying bits of foreground material on the background and pinning them in place. At this stage it all sprang to life.

When the design was finished, a much smaller group of two or three continued in the next session, starting to sew them on. At the end it was easier for one person (the leader) to finish it off at home. This finishing work included sewing on a backing sheet, sewing loops at the top for hanging, and ironing it flat.

Preparing the readings

There were two sessions of 4 and 6 people, each concentrating on one reading: an Old Testament reading of Malachi 3:1–5 and a Gospel reading of Luke 2:22–40. Each session began with some background theology, especially the theme that, though Christ was the light of the world, that light was to be extinguished, if only temporarily. Candlemas marks the transition from the joy of his birth to the anticipation of his death. The groups split the text so that each person had something to read.

Poetry and psalm writing

On a weekend at Lee Abbey, the leader had taken part in a workshop in which the participants had been encouraged to express their prayers and thoughts in the form of a psalm. Mostly, they produced verse which was very free, and hardly any psalm form at all. Having been through this once himself, he volunteered to try leading the activity. It was considerably more difficult than he imagined!

This was a popular activity, so he had to run it twice. On the first occasion, people split into ones and twos to write. This worked for some individuals and pairs, but others had

problems. He found that two different groups of two young-
sters each seemed to need more of his attention than he had to
spare from the other pair. This caused him to change his
method in the second session, so that they stayed together and
worked as one group. With two very helpful adults in the
group who contributed a lot, this worked well. The psalm they
wrote, which was in line with the theme of the whole day, was
published in the parish magazine.

Two of the groups in the first session looked at the psalms
and tried to write poetry in the form of a psalm. As
Candlemas is the time when we celebrate the presentation of
Jesus in the temple, they thought about what it might have
been like for Jesus to be growing up, looking forward to adult
life, and what it is like for us. The following psalm was
written by a group of five people:

What will I be when I grow up? What shall I do when I am
older?
Shall I be a doctor, and heal the sick, a dentist, and care
for people's teeth?
Shall I work in an office, shall I be a secretary or an accoun-
tant?
Shall I be a teacher or a nanny, and care for the children?
What shall I do when I am older? What will I be when I grow
up?
What did Jesus think he would be? What would he do when
he was older?
Did he want to be a carpenter, and praise God with his hands?
Did he want to be a priest, and praise God in his temple?
When Jesus was older, what did he do? What was he when
he grew up?
He was a teacher, and taught the people. He was a healer,
and healed the sick.
He cared for God's children; he fed them and told them
stories.
What will I be when I grow up? What shall I do when I am
older?
God showed Jesus the way to go. He will show the way for
me.

Liturgical dancing

The members of this group devised a dance to the song 'Shine Jesus Shine', with some people dancing with the candles that they had made or decorated earlier. Although everyone had agreed at the outset that with a single session there would not be adequate time to prepare a dance for the Sunday service, by the end of the session all the dancers wanted to have an opportunity to show what they had done. As not everyone could be at the Sunday service, they performed their dance at the Service of Light.

Bible study

This was a small group. The leader had prepared a simple outline which took the group through Luke 2:22–40. The passage provoked so much discussion that the end was not reached.

The group included a wide age range but worked well using the method of splitting into pairs to discuss topics, then coming back into a single group to share. This overcame the embarrassment some felt at speaking out in a group.

Preparing the intercessions

This was also a small group, and the leader felt the participants knew as much about preparing intercessions as he did. *The Alternative Service Book 1980* rite A structure was followed, with the sections divided among the participants. The working time felt rushed and not very prayerful, but it all came together in the end. The result was written out for the service, with each person reading the section they had prepared.

How: Sunday morning worship

The order of service for the 9.30 Sunday morning service was rite A communion service from *The Alternative Service Book 1980*, with additions from *The Promise of His Glory*.

Candles were handed to the congregation on arrival. The relevant activity groups led the Old Testament and Gospel readings, the intercessions and the gradual hymn. Instead of a sermon the activity groups not otherwise involved in leading parts of the service gave short accounts of what they had done: the banner was displayed, church decorations were pointed out, rolls from the baking group were shown and two poems were read. After the communion came the Candlemas procession, in which the congregation sang a hymn while candles were lit throughout the church by members of the candle making group, using the candles they had made.

Evaluation

The workshop was generally agreed to be very successful. Between 40 and 50 people came, over half of them children. A typical remark was 'Why don't we do this more often?'

Trying to arrange the sessions to suit everyone on the basis of slips returned beforehand was a headache which was not really justified as last minute changes had to be made in any case; no one was turned away because they had not returned a slip.

As was expected, the activities varied in popularity. Some activities did not attract young children at all. Some activities were not popular with the teenagers, though candle making proved to be a great success. On reflection, there was not a big enough choice of activities for the numbers of young children, so some activities were very crowded while others had plenty of places available.

Tea, biscuits and squash were provided in the hall between sessions, but some group leaders missed out because they were too busy clearing up from one group and getting ready for the next one.

The workshop did not break even financially, in that the hire of the school was paid for directly out of parish funds. It would have been better to make a fixed charge of £1 per person.

The timetable worked well, except that there was not enough time in church for the run through of the following day's service. The commitment to the morning service the following day was stressful and demanding, more so because in some ways it was a 'presentation' to those who had not participated in the workshops on Saturday as well as to those who had.

It was agreed that the things that would be done differently when the next similar event happened would be:

to hold the event on a Sunday after the 9.30 service;

to provide lunch at a cost of £1 per person;

to keep the event separate from formal service in the church, but to keep a closing act of worship in the school at which each group could contribute;

participation in group work to be decided by signing up on arrival on a 'first come, first served' basis, which would solve the difficulties over slips not sent in advance but would also mean that group leaders would have no idea whether or not their groups would be full.

Resources

Songs

Christ, whose glory fills the skies (*Hymns Ancient and Modern New Standard* 4)

Thou whose almighty word (*Hymns Ancient and Modern New Standard* 180)

The holly and the ivy (*Come and Praise* 119)

Bible

Malachi 3:1–5 (Prophecy of the Lord coming to the temple)

Luke 2:22–40 (Presentation of Christ in the temple)

Books

The Promise of His Glory, London, Church House Publishing, 1991

F L Cross (ed.), *The Oxford Dictionary of the Christian Church*, Oxford, Oxford University Press, 1974

Michael Perham and Kenneth Stevenson, *Welcoming the Light of Christ*, London, SPCK, 1991.

2 STATIONS OF THE CROSS

Anne Thorne

Why

Each year the people of St James, Exeter, have run a Lent course for the children using a different theme. This year we chose to use the *Stations of the Cross* in order to give background information to the children on the last week of our Lord's life. Each year we hold a stations of the cross service for children on Good Friday. This year we wanted to explain to the children the story behind each station, so that when they attended the Good Friday service they would have time to reflect on what actually happened, the feelings and thoughts of those people we hear so much about at Easter.

Where

St James is a modern building with movable chairs. Using the church meant that the children could look at our own stations of the cross situated around the building, and perhaps for the first time really understand what they meant.

When

On five consecutive Thursday evenings during Lent, we met from 5.30 until 6.30 in the church. On Maundy Thursday we met during the morning from 9.30 until 11.30 in the church hall.

How: publicity

Publicity was through the parish magazine and the weekly news sheet. The church has a large Sunday school and letters containing details were sent home with the children. Posters were put up in the local first and middle schools.

How: programme

The stations were split up into six sessions. These would be followed by the Good Friday service.

Week 1	Jesus is condemned and receives his cross
Week 2	Jesus' journey
Week 3	People Jesus met on the way
Week 4	Jesus dies
Week 5	The burial of Jesus
Week 6	New life
Good Friday	Stations of the cross service

How: the course

Each session followed a similar pattern. We started with a hymn and a prayer. We chose to use only four hymns throughout the six weeks, learning a new verse of each hymn each week. Every session included a relevant discussion, an activity and a game where possible, ending with a hymn and a prayer. At the end of each session the children took home a picture to colour in and a memory verse to colour and learn, based on that week's theme. We organised a colouring competition with weekly prizes for the best memory verse and the best picture.

Week one

The session began with a prayer and the singing of 'Go tell it on the mountain'. The children then coloured this week's memory verse which was, 'Pilate said "There is nothing this man has done to deserve death"' (Luke 23:15). A short sketch was performed, showing how Pilate washed his hands of the whole affair.

The children played 'Simon says'. This game helped them to see how easy it is to be carried away by copying others (in this case 'Simon'), and the necessity to do what you think is right. A brief discussion followed this on the importance of making their own decisions.

After singing 'Jesus died for all the children', each child was given an outline of a cross drawn on a piece of A4 card. These cross outlines were filled in and covered with faces cut out from magazines. This was to illustrate that Jesus died on the cross for everyone, no matter what age, colour, race or creed.

We explained to the children that Jesus carried just the cross piece of his cross, and then invited them to feel the weight of a cross which the rector had made out of two pieces of wood, the first piece 2 m by 15 cm and the second piece 1 m by 15 cm. This cross was tied to a stall at the chancel step and remained there throughout Lent.

We finished with the hymn 'There is a green hill far away' and a closing prayer. The children were then given a picture to take home and colour in. This first week's picture was of Pilate washing his hands.

Week two

The theme of the second week was Jesus' journey. The memory verse was 'He went out carrying his cross and came to The Place of the Skull' (John 19:17).

After a review of the previous week, we talked with the children about journeys they had made: exciting, boring, happy, sad and scary ones. We discussed Jesus' journey, talked about the weight of the cross and how they thought Jesus felt both physically and mentally.

The children then heard an 'eye witness' account of Jesus' journey. This story was taken from the Scripture Union *Learning Together* series April–June 1992.

The activity for this week was to make silhouette posters of Jesus' journey on pieces of A4 size white card. The children cut out from black card (using templates if they chose) pictures of crosses, hills, clouds and tears.

The children greatly enjoyed making the noises they might have heard on Jesus' journey. There were people crying, soldiers marching, the crowd talking, stones crunching underfoot, the cross being dragged. These noises were then taped onto a cassette and played back to the children.

The take home colouring picture for the week was of people watching Jesus on his journey.

Week three

The theme for this week was people Jesus met on the way. The chosen memory verse was 'Women of Jerusalem! Don't cry for me, but for yourselves and your children' (Luke 23:28). We then spent some time talking about each of the different people Jesus met on the way: Simon, Mary, the women of Jerusalem and Veronica.

The younger children's activity was about the legend of Veronica and involved drawing a picture of the impression that was left on Veronica's cloth. The older children pretended they were Simon and wrote a letter home to their family telling what had just happened to them.

A true/false game was played outside. One side of the garden was designated true and the other false. Statements about bible events were read out to the children and they moved to the true or false side of the garden. The aim of the game was to show how easily we can be influenced by what other people think and do, and so it was important to include some statements that the children did not know. We found if one child was positive and moved to a chosen side, many other children would move to that same side, even if they did not understand the question. It gave us the chance to discuss the importance of thinking for ourselves and not being influenced by others.

We finished with a hymn and a prayer. The children were given a take home colouring picture of Jesus carrying his cross as he walked past Mary.

Week four

After the opening prayers and hymns, we reviewed the previous three weeks to see how much the children could remember. We also gave prizes to the children who could remember all three memory verses.

This week's memory verse was 'Jesus cried out in a loud voice, "Father! In your hands I place my spirit!" He said this and died' (Luke 23:46). We talked with the children about what this verse might mean, then discussed events such as the thieves who were crucified with Jesus, the spear in his side, the blood and water, and the curtain in the temple.

Each child was given a piece of A4 paper with the outline of a large nail drawn on it. In the middle of the nail they wrote many things we do that are wrong. These nails were then cut out and attached to the large wooden cross and displayed in church throughout the rest of Lent.

We discussed with the children the burial of Jesus, why he would have been buried in a tomb and not a grave, and why spices were used.

The session was drawn to a close with the singing of a hymn and a prayer, and the children were given their take home colouring picture, which was the crowd standing round watching Jesus die on the cross.

Week five

We started with a prayer and hymn. By week five the children were well into the routine and enjoyed reviewing the last few weeks and between them remembering even the smallest details. The children coloured in this week's memory verse which was 'The women who had followed Jesus from Galilee went with Joseph and saw the tomb and how Jesus' body was placed in it' (Luke 23:55).

We sang the hymn 'Were you there when they crucified my Lord?'

The next activity had the children on the edge of their seats with anticipation. Before the session a balloon had been filled with lots of tiny pieces of paper. One person read out some facts about Jesus' life, and each time a fact was read out the balloon was blown up a bit more. As the balloon grew and grew the children became more and more excited. After the last statement was read out the balloon was suddenly and unexpectedly popped with a pin. All the little pieces of paper inside scattered everywhere, which led on to us explaining that although the balloon looks dead it has scattered all the pieces of paper. In just the same way, when Jesus died and rose again the Holy Spirit was released to each of us. (The children had great fun trying to pick up all the pieces of paper again.)

The children were given their take home picture, which for this week was Jesus being carried to the tomb.

Week six

This week's memory verse was 'I have come in order that you might have life' (John 10:10).

We reviewed the last five weeks, then the children coloured in this week's memory verse and picture, so that all their verses and pictures could be put together to make a book for each child. We held a competition for the best book.

We discussed things not being what they seem and talked about the balloon from last week. Then an egg was cracked over someone's head, one that had been previously blown, another example of things not being what they seem.

The children planted cress seeds in the shape of a cross on cotton wool placed on paper plates. These were taken home, again to show that though the seeds look dead, in fact they are full of life.

The whole course ended with each child making paper flowers out of white, yellow, cream and green crêpe paper, tissue paper and card. On Easter Saturday when the Easter Garden was laid out in church, the children helped take their nails off the large cross and replace them with the flowers. On Easter Sunday this cross had pride of place in the middle of the high altar and many of the congregation commented on how lovely it was.

We ended with a hymn and a prayer and each child was invited to join in the stations of the cross service which was to take place the next day.

Good Friday

On Good Friday we held our stations of the cross service using the hymns the children had learnt during the Lent course, followed by a drink and hot cross buns in the church hall.

We had planned to hold this Good Friday *Way of the Cross* service outside the church, with very simple stations drawn on A3 card, hoping that this would make the children more aware of the reality of the way of the cross for our Lord. Unfortunately bad weather prevented this and we held the service inside.

Evaluation

We found the use of a plain wooden cross very effective. This was tied to a stall at the chancel step and in full view during all our services on Sundays and weekdays. Starting off bare, it became more impressive when covered with the 'nails' on which the children had written the names of various sins. Its complete transformation, which was carried out on Holy Saturday by replacing the ugly 'nails' with brightly coloured tissue flowers, made a dramatic impression on adults and children alike when it replaced the crucifix on the high altar for the whole of Easter week.

Resources

Songs

Go tell it on the mountain (*Junior Praise* 65)
Jesus died for all the children (*Junior Praise* 132)
There is a green hill far away (*Junior Praise* 245)
Were you there when they crucified my Lord? (*Junior Praise* 269)

Bible

Luke 23:15 (Pilate's verdict)
Luke 23:28 (Women of Jerusalem)
Luke 23:46 (Jesus' death)
John 19:17 (Jesus carries the cross)
Luke 23:55 (Jesus' burial)
John 10:10 (Jesus' promise of life)

3 WAY OF THE CROSS

Stephen Cottrell

Why

Central to the presentation of the Christian faith is the cross of Jesus Christ. It is all too easy for children within the church to grow up learning a lot about the birth of Jesus, about his teaching, healing, feeding, and about God raising him from death, but knowing very little about Good Friday. Like those adults who sing 'Hosanna' on Palm Sunday and 'Alleluia' on Easter Day, but do not come to church on Good Friday, our children may only think of this day in terms of hot cross buns. At our church we decided that to present the full challenge of the Christian faith, we had to bring children to the foot of the cross.

We chose to do this by breathing new life into the ancient service of the *Stations of the Cross*. This devotion began in Jerusalem where pilgrims would follow the route of Jesus' last journey from Pilate's palace to Calvary. Certain stops were made on the route to reflect on particular incidents on the journey which are recorded in scripture and remembered in the tradition. Under the influence of Saint Francis of Assisi these 'stations' were re-created through paintings and statues in local churches so that people who never dreamt of being able to visit Jerusalem could experience, through prayer and praise, something of the strength and majesty of this hard journey.

Many cathedrals and churches now have stations of the cross around their walls. Particularly during Lent Christian people follow the stations and meditate on the last hours of Jesus' life on earth.

Where

The church of St Wilfrid's, Parklands, where this took place
is a small council estate parish on the edge of the prosperous
city of Chichester. It has a well equipped modern hall and
small meeting rooms adjacent to the church building. We used
all the facilities of church and hall and the grounds outside to
re-create our journey.

When

On five consecutive Tuesdays during Lent we met for an hour
after school between 3.30 and 4.30. We regularly have an
after school children's club, called *Icthus*, meeting at this time
with a specific aim of introducing the Christian faith to children outside, as well as inside, the worshipping life of the
church. Such a group could, however, be set up specifically
for a Lenten children's exercise.

The *Icthus* club attracts children from several different
schools. This means that the children do not all arrive at the
same time and need some space each week to greet each other
before the session begins. We allow for this by providing
drinks and biscuits and by playing games until everyone has
arrived.

The last of the Tuesdays was in Holy Week. On that occasion we held an act of worship to which families, friends and
the whole church were invited.

How: publicity

Initial publicity was given through the church newsletter
which was delivered to every home in the parish, through
posters displayed in local shops and through contact in local
schools. The publicity made it clear that the activities were
designed primarily for 5–11 year olds.

How: planning

A small group of two adults and two teenagers got together to look at the images of the stations of the cross and to explore the biblical foundations on which they are set. Traditionally there are 14 stations, though nowadays a further one is often added:

1. Pontius Pilate condemns Jesus to death (John 19:4–11, 16);
2. Jesus receives his cross (Matthew 11:29–30);
3. Jesus falls for the first time (Isaiah 53:4–8);
4. Jesus meets Mary his mother (Song of Songs 3:1–4);
5. Simon of Cyrene helps Jesus to carry the cross (Mark 15:16);
6. Veronica wipes the face of Jesus (Matthew 25:35–40);
7. Jesus falls for the second time (Philippians 2:6–7);
8. Jesus meets the women of Jerusalem (Luke 23:27–28);
9. Jesus falls for the third time (Psalm 88:1–4);
10. Jesus is stripped of his garments (John 19:23–24);
11. Jesus is nailed to the cross (Luke 23:33–34);
12. Jesus dies on the cross (Luke 23:44–46);
13. Jesus is taken down from the cross (1 John 4:9–11);
14. Jesus is laid in the tomb (Mark 15:42–47);
15. Jesus is risen (1 Corinthians 15:12–22).

From these 15 stations we selected three themes: the journey itself; the people who met Jesus on the way and who helped him; and the sense of Jesus sharing in the sadness of life through his way of the cross.

From a number of devotional books written on the stations of the cross, some of which are listed in the Resources, we looked at different pictures, discussed their impact and chose a short sentence of scripture to accompany each station. We were keen to explore our themes by finding ways of presenting the feelings of Jesus on his journey through pictures, movement and song. We went away to think and pray about it all.

At a second meeting we decided which stations we would deal with each week and how to structure each session. We then divided up responsibilities and made our final plans.

Appeal was made to the congregation for all sorts of collage materials from which we would make the pictures of the stations. A member of the church who was skilled in wood-work was asked to make a cross for one of the children to carry. Another person wrote a song which was to be sung as we walked from one station to the next (see Appendix).

How: the first four weeks

The process

After the drink and biscuit and game, each session followed a similar pattern. First we told the story of the stations we were covering. Then a song helped us get inside the feelings of the events, and drama helped us bring the actions to life. The children would then be ready to express their own responses to the stations through artwork. Each week we made large collages of the different stations. This was the central activity. Each session ended with prayer. This helped focus our hearts and minds on God's purpose and love shown us, so intensely, in the cross of Jesus.

The songs which were sung each week and then used in the service were either written specially or chosen as ones the children might already know. Suggestions are listed in the Resources. Putting your own words to well known tunes is, however, a more exciting way of getting the right mood for a particular service and is to be encouraged. The 'Follow me, follow' song was learnt by heart and given actions. It became the theme song and was sung each week.

For the drama one child was chosen to represent Jesus and simple mimed actions were devised to illustrate the different stages of the journey. Most weeks the leading players in the drama stayed on a while to practise as the others split into groups to make the stations.

The making of the collages of the stations had to be very carefully planned since there were fairly large numbers of children all working on only a couple of pictures. Splitting them into groups, they worked at different tables on different parts of the picture which were then all put together on large pieces of card. Mostly the pictures just depicted that bit of the story we were dealing with but, as I have indicated, they also managed to get inside the story by revealing truths in a challenging visual image. As is often the case, the children themselves had many of the best ideas.

It was important to have a wide selection of materials and plenty of scissors and pens and glue so that each child could get straight on with his or her bit of the picture. We always gave ourselves at least half an hour for this activity. The finished pictures looked magnificent.

As the groups of children finished their artwork they were gathered into prayer groups to write prayers and meditations based on the different stations. These were then used at the final session of sharing before going home.

Week one

The first week we looked at stations one and two: Pontius Pilate condemns Jesus to death and Jesus receives his cross. In the story time we thought about the silence of Jesus before his accusers and the false charge brought against him. We thought about Pilate washing his hands of Jesus and how sometimes we look for easy ways out of difficult situations. We talked about the weight of the cross and brought in two large planks to illustrate the sheer heaviness of it. We discussed how Jesus in his life and death shares our life and death.

The picture of Jesus carrying the cross sought to express this visually. A collage of the cross was made from lots of faces cut from magazines.

Week two

The following week we looked at stations four, five and six: the people Jesus encountered on the way, these being his mother, Simon of Cyrene and Veronica. In the story time we thought of how sad Mary must have been to see Jesus carrying his cross. A child's perspective on this is interesting to note. 'Thank you for letting Jesus see his mother before he died,' wrote one in the prayer time at the end.

We thought about how hard it is for us to think about people we love dying. We thought how brave Simon and Veronica must have been to offer Jesus help. We wondered how we might help Jesus today by helping one another.

In the legend of Veronica wiping the face of Jesus there is a lovely tradition that the imprint of Jesus' face was left on the cloth. We thought how as we grow older our faces express what kind of people we are. We looked at different pictures of the face of Jesus and then drew our own which were incorporated into this week's collages. We listed different words to describe the character of Jesus.

The prayers and meditations written at the end of the session showed how much the children were entering into the experience of the story. 'My name is Simon,' wrote one, 'I come from Cyrene. One day I saw a terrible scene. It was a man with a wooden cross. He fell. I rushed through the crowd and offered him my help. He was very pleased to rest for a while. He gave me a smile.'

Week three

In the third week we looked at stations twelve and fourteen: Jesus dies on the cross and Jesus is laid in the tomb. In the story time we talked about how painful the cross must have been. We spoke of the burden of sin Jesus was carrying and of his dying to forgive us and how he was sharing our life on earth so that we might share his life in heaven. We thought about the words Jesus spoke from the cross, especially: 'Father, forgive them, they do not know what they are doing' (Luke 23:34) and, to the penitent thief, 'Today you will be with me in paradise' (Luke 23:43).

These are difficult ideas for any age group to deal with. However, the depth of a child's understanding is well illustrated by this prayer written by a seven year old: 'Dear Jesus, thank you for dying on the cross because you loved us so much. But we are glad you rose from the dead because you loved us so, so much. And we are very sorry you died on the cross, but we are very glad that you made a path to heaven.'

We made paper nails and wrote on them something we had done wrong. We stuck these around our collage of Jesus on the cross.

In the prayers some of us imagined Jesus speaking to us from the cross today.

Week four

In the last week we looked at the last station: Jesus is risen. In the story time we talked about how sad the friends of Jesus must have been when he died and how frightened they were when they first saw him alive; they thought he was a ghost. We talked about how happy they must have been when they realised what the Resurrection meant, that out of death comes life. We talked about how things are not always what they seem. We went outside and looked at the signs of spring all around us, how an apparently dead earth was springing to life. We read the scripture 'Unless a grain of wheat falls on the ground and dies it remains a single grain; but if it dies it yields a rich harvest' (John 12:24).

We looked at pictures of the cross which have flowers blooming from those very places where the nails had been. We talked about the new life which Jesus makes available to all and mentioned baptism, where we go down into the waters, a death, and rise up again, a resurrection.

The activities this week had to be a little different since there was a need to rehearse actions and prayers for the service the following week. All the children made a flower as a symbol of the resurrection, using for the stem a paper nail like the ones made the previous week to surround the picture of the death of Jesus. The younger ones then made a simple Easter garden with stones and little wooden crosses, moss and flowers which had been collected beforehand. The rest of the children went through a rehearsal for the service.

How: week five

Week five was an act of worship called 'A way of the cross for children'. About thirty children had attended the first four weeks, so now we were joined by a large crowd of mums and dads, brothers and sisters, grandparents and other members of the church and even an interested teacher from one of the children's schools who had been told about the project. Our journey began in the hall and the stations were arranged along a route which took us through the hall, outside, into the church and finished at the Easter garden which was placed at the foot of the altar.

One of the adults introduced the service and said a very brief word at each station. A child announced the name of the station and there was a short responsory, taken from *Lent, Holy Week and Easter*, p. 96:

Leader   We adore you, Christ, and we bless you;
Everyone   because by your holy cross you have redeemed
           the world.

This was said at each station. Another child read a sentence from scripture. A brief word of explanation was given and then the drama was performed. A song, or a verse from a song, was sung and then one or two children read out their prayer or meditation. We then moved on to the next station singing 'Follow me, follow' behind the child carrying the cross.

Everyone had a special sheet with the names of the stations, words of the responsory and songs on it. The children's prayers were also typed onto a sheet and afterwards everyone was given a copy to take home.

At the final station we all stood around the Easter garden holding our flowers and singing 'What a friend we have in Jesus'. We then all shared a drink and a hot cross bun. This time we hoped the symbol on the bun meant something real to the child.

Evaluation

The stations of the cross are often thought of as an adult form of worship because they involve silence and reflection. We discovered them to be an ideal form of worship for children. Those elements of the journey – movement, picture and song – which so captured their imagination were the perfect way of leading them to think creatively about the cross and also encouraged an environment of silence and prayer which was beautiful to experience.

Let me give the final word to one of the children. This simple and striking prayer is the best illustration of how profound a child's faith can be when given space to grow. It was written by an eight year old.

'Dear Jesus, thank you for dying for us. Help us to stop putting nails in your cross.'

Appendix

Processional song

Follow me, follow – on the way of Jesus,
He is my brother, he is my friend.
Follow me, follow – on the way of Jesus,
Carry the cross of love.

Resources

Songs

Amazing grace (*Junior Praise* 8)
Be still and know that I am God (*Junior Praise* 22)
Father I place into your hands (*Junior Praise* 42)
I met you at the cross (*Junior Praise* 103)
Jesus died for all the children (*Junior Praise* 132)
Jesus remember me (*Taize*)
Kumbaya (*Junior Praise* 149)
O Lord hear my prayer (*Taize*)
On Calvary's tree he died for me (*Junior Praise* 183)
Shalom my friend (*Junior Praise* 217)
There is a green hill far away (*Junior Praise* 245)
Were you there when they crucified my Lord? (*Junior Praise* 269)
What a friend we have in Jesus (*Junior Praise* 273)

Bible

Psalm 88:1–4 (Jesus falls for the third time)
Song of Songs 3:1–4 (Jesus meets Mary his mother)
Isaiah 53:4–8 (Jesus falls for the first time)
Matthew 11:29–30 (Jesus receives his cross)
Matthew 25:35–40 (Veronica wipes the face of Jesus)
Mark 15:16 (Simon of Cyrene helps Jesus to carry the cross)
Mark 15:42–47 (Jesus is laid in the tomb)
Luke 23:27–28 (Jesus meets the women of Jerusalem)
Luke 23:33–34 (Jesus is nailed to the cross)
Luke 23:44–46 (Jesus dies on the cross)
John 19:4–11, 16 (Pontius Pilate condemns Jesus to death)
John 19:23–24 (Jesus is stripped of his garments)
1 Corinthians 15:12–22 (Jesus is risen)
Philippians 2:6–7 (Jesus falls for the second time)
1 John 4:9–11 (Jesus is taken down from the cross)

Books

Peter Cullen, *The Stations of the Cross*, Great Wakering, McCrimmon Publishing, 1981 (a set of posters is also available to accompany this booklet)
H J Richards, *A Way of the Cross for Children*, Great Wakering, McCrimmon Publishing, 1986

4 DEANERY PENTECOST

Anne Faulkner

Why

The education committee of the Deanery Synod was set up to help churches implement the General Synod report, *Children in the Way*. A survey carried out in the churches of the deanery showed that most churches would like the experience of an all age day, but did not feel confident enough to run their own. This committee therefore chose to organise an all age day for all churches of the deanery.

The day would have several aims. One aim would be to give those attending a good experience. Another aim would be to give them the confidence to plan such an event in their own area or parish in the future. A third aim would be to generate a higher profile to the idea of all ages learning together.

Where

This is a deanery of contrasts: the affluent commuter villages and the poverty of some estates; the leafy green of dense woods and the chimneys of the industrial estates; the river winding through the fields and the decomposing cars in front gardens. The people are varied too: all colours, all religions and all cultures. Hindus, Moslems, Sikhs and Christians attempt to live side by side, along with the greater number of those who are not affiliated with any group.

The deanery mirrors the wider church in its variety of approaches to, and practice of, leadership in the local churches. In some churches lay people respond to the opportunities offered to them to receive training and to take up different leadership roles; in some churches lay people are not given much chance to lead; in other churches lay people are not willing, able or confident enough to train or to take a leadership part in the life of their church.

In many churches in the deanery there is a lively approach to liturgy. In older church buildings the traditional and the modern, the formal and the informal sit side by side with varying degrees of comfort. In other places there is less tradition of liturgy and so there is more scope for informality and experiment in worship.

There is very little contact between the parishes of the deanery, except at synodical level where a small handful of individuals know other individuals well. The one exception to this is the network of teenagers and young people who meet several times a year on Sunday evenings for deanery youth services which are sometimes followed by social events.

When

Pentecost seemed a good time for an all age day with a theme of the Holy Spirit. This would give plenty of scope for activities, games and worship with the symbols of wind and fire. Pentecost is a festival that is often regarded in churches as difficult, so a day such as this could also be used in the worship in local churches on Pentecost Sunday. The Saturday a week before Pentecost was chosen.

The day was planned to begin at 10.00 and carefully structured to close at 4.00.

How: planning

The planning group consisted of the education committee and one of the diocesan advisors. Although this only represented five congregations in the deanery, there was a commitment from the beginning to include many others, from as wide an age range as possible, in leading the event.

The first meeting of the planning group was held about five months before the event. Because it was a deanery event, it would take time to communicate with the different churches, and even more time for the news and the information to reach the members of the congregations.

From the start, key issues were the involvement of as many people as possible in leading the day, the booking of people and places, and the publicity to the thirty or so Anglican churches of the deanery, as well as other denominations. The planning group set out to address these issues, as well as to attend to the finer points of detail in the programme.

Four planning meetings were held, followed by an on-site briefing meeting for all those with any duties on the day. Each member of the planning group undertook an area of responsibility, recruiting and training a team to assist. These areas of responsibility included activities, worship, equipment and furniture, food and drink, publicity and finance. This involved a large number of people from all parts of the deanery, and was helpful in publicising the day.

Planning the venue involved many factors. The majority of the church buildings in the deanery are old and traditional in architectural style; they have heavy pews, mainly fixed to the floor, and very little clear space. A conscious decision was made to hold this day in one such venue, although not ideal and rather inconvenient, rather than in a modern church with chairs that are movable, with carpeted areas and with good amenities. In this way others could imitate the event, however difficult they perceived their own church buildings to be. Priority was given to finding a venue with wheelchair access and one which was safe from the road and from intruders so that the children had some freedom. The church selected was fairly small with fixed seating and a raised chancel. There was a hall next door with a kitchen and toilets, a drive and a space for parking, as well as a piece of grass.

Plans were made for any weather. There was space in the church for activities to be housed indoors in the event of rain, but there was scope to spill outside on the grass. With a little imagination it was discovered that even this church, the most unpromising of buildings, could be adapted. The choir stalls, which were screwed to the floor, could be removed to give space to the dance group. The icon painting group could find the peace that it required in the unused, second church porch. Easels for painting could be put outside on the grass in fine weather, so that those who wished could paint in peace and make as much mess as they liked. Side doors to the hall opened onto the grass, so it was possible for modelling to start inside but to spill outside. Two small quiet vestries could be home to the instrumental group and to the four part singing group, as a space of their own is a must for such groups.

How: publicity

Posters, leaflets and handbills were produced by the planning group. All age participation was stressed in the publicity. The printed forms included a return slip indicating the need to know in advance the numbers and approximate ages of those planning to attend.

The publicity materials were distributed via helpers, clergy and Deanery Synod members. As the planning group did not want the day to be perceived as a children's day, the network of Sunday school teachers and junior church leaders was *not* used.

Some churches already had experience of children's days and children's holiday activities and clubs. It was important for them to understand the thinking behind the idea of an all age experience and the aim of this day. In some places this meant a hard sell of the idea of an all age day. This took place informally with individuals and small groups.

How: finance

The Deanery Synod gave the venture its support and its money, as there was much equipment needed. Some of this equipment was lent by churches, and everyone was asked to bring a pair of named scissors with them, but some things had to be bought, like clay and paint.

How: programme

The following programme provided the basic framework.

10.00	Arrival and welcome (*hall*)
	Tea/coffee/squash
	Make a label
	Graffiti board
10.15	Bonfire and parachute games (*outside*)
10.45	Graffiti board reflection on bonfire and parachute experience (*church*)
	Story of first Pentecost (Acts 2)
11.00	Selection of activity groups (*church*)
11.05	Activity groups (*everywhere*)
12.30	Lunch (*hall/outside*)
1.00	Activity groups (*everywhere*)
2.30	Tea/coffee/squash (*moving to church*)
	Preparation for closing eucharist
3.00	Eucharist (*church*)
3.45	Tea – with Pentecost cake for the church's birthday (*hall*)
4.00	Finish

How: opening

There was much setting up to do in advance so helpers arrived early. As well as moving furniture and preparing activities, toilets had to be signposted, a first aid post set up, emergency exits labelled and a car park attendant briefed.

By 9.45 people began to arrive and the day was under way.

On arrival, the first thing people saw was a large graffiti board of newsprint pinned to a long wall, headed with the questions, 'What is Pentecost? What does it mean to me?' Quite quickly a collection of words, images and pictures appeared on the wall. Everyone talked together as they filled in the board, drank their coffee and made labels to wear.

Next came experiences of fire and of wind, two of the traditional symbols of the Holy Spirit. A bonfire had been prepared, complete with a safety barrier. The fire was lit with a cheer and the spontaneous, unplanned singing of 'Camp fires burning'. Children and adults alike were happy to watch the fire grow and burn for ten or fifteen minutes. When attention began to waver, a parachute was produced on the grass well away from the fire and simple games were played, such as changing places beneath the parachute as it billows up, and making a Mexican wave that goes round the circle. The parachute made a wonderful wind for all to feel.

One of the strengths of parachute games is that people of all ages, sizes and abilities can join in. Quite small children can stand with elderly adults; people in wheelchairs or sitting on chairs are able to be part of the fun; those who cannot see or hear well are not disadvantaged. Parachutes can be bought especially for playing games, but if you are fortunate you may manage to get an ex-RAF aviation parachute.

At 10.45, the graffiti board was taken into church with everyone following. People were asked to reflect on their experience of the fire of the bonfire and the wind of the parachute, and then to call out further words and images to add to those already on the board. The story of the first Pentecost in The Acts of the Apostles chapter 2 was told.

How: activities

Activity groups occupied much of the rest of the day. The menu of activities was wide and all were linked to the theme of wind and fire in some way. These groups had been planned to meet a variety of needs for different age and interest groups. Individuals made their own choices about how long they remained with an activity. Some people of varying ages only tried two activities, one in the morning and one in the afternoon. Those who opted to do icon painting remained absorbed all day, oblivious to the delights of other activities. Others moved from one place to another and managed to try most things that were on offer. One or two more restless people needed a little encouragement to settle down to a group, but there was plenty to choose from. A few adults were available to channel the more reluctant or confused participants into an activity.

Art and craft

Several different art and craft activities were provided. There was free painting to express wind and fire, as well as more directed pictures of bonfires, kites, and other aspects of the Pentecost theme. Red, yellow and orange paper cut into strips and bound to a small garden cane made excellent fire streamers. Paper collage was used to make large banners to carry in procession and to prop up round the church walls. Some adults discovered the delights of the new experience of cutting and sticking paper. An altar frontal showing tongues of fire was sewn in coloured felt, decorated with sequins and gold beads, by children and adults, male and female. Some remained in this sewing group all day, others came and went. Each time someone different arrived there was much discussion about the design.

Modelling

Both junk modelling and clay modelling are messy and need much space. This activity group, led by three young teenagers, was located outside next to the free painting so that the models could be easily painted, clay and hands could be dipped in water without worry, and the mess could be kept to a minimum.

Children and adults worked well together, with many of the children able to teach the adults how to use clay. Kite making and windmills appealed mostly to the young or the young at heart. Two men, using the excuse of 'helping the children', spent the entire afternoon experimenting with the length and the nature of the tail of a kite to try to improve its performance. Probably the most popular activity was boat making, using scraps of wood from a timber yard and from people's garages. All ages, male and female, spent a long time cutting, sanding, constructing and painting boats of all shapes and kinds, then floating the boats in the paddling pool provided, and making necessary improvements.

This was one of the best examples of an activity where people of all ages can work together, discussing and learning from each other. Some people remained in this group for all the time available.

Cooking

Cooking was a popular activity and fortunately the hall kitchen was not too small. The morning session was spent making small cakes to distribute at lunch time, and making the bread, from a bread mix, for the closing eucharist. In the afternoon session four large oblong cakes were made, put together on a board and decorated as one very big birthday cake complete with candles, to celebrate Pentecost as the birthday of the church.

Music

Four different types of music activities tried to accommodate the interests of as many people as possible. In the morning session the two leaders offered fun singing, attended mostly by children, and instrumental playing for those who had responded to the invitation to bring musical instruments with them. The instruments brought on the day included clarinets, violins and flutes. In the afternoon two more music activities were offered: percussion for fun and four part singing. All of these activities made some contribution to the closing eucharist. With the exception of the fun singing they all attracted participants from a wide age range.

Dance

The dance group met in the afternoon to dance the story of the day of Pentecost as recorded in the Acts of the Apostles. This activity attracted a great number of female dancers and one or two brave men. Small children did not find it easy but there was plenty of help available. The dancers chose to use some of the streamers made by the art and craft group.

Prayer

Two different prayer activities were offered. One, origami, involved folding paper doves, then writing on their wings prayers for guidance of the Holy Spirit. This involved much discussion and thought. The second activity, icon painting, appealed to people's curiosity. This ancient form of prayer was greatly simplified for the purposes of the occasion, but still took all day to complete. The icons of Pentecost were prayerfully painted on blocks of wood by a small group of adults and older teenagers.

Science

Simple experiments with fire, air and wind attracted people all day. These were held inside the hall, with carefully observed safety regulations.

Other activities

Puzzles, word games and word searches were available in one corner to give a chance for some peace and quiet for those who wanted it. Two 400 piece jigsaws, linked to the theme, kept some people occupied for hours. Others came to give advice or to put in one or two pieces, and then moved on. The book corner was not much used, but was appreciated by a few. A carpet with toys for the 'tinies' proved to be an attraction to older children too.

How: worship

Children and adults brought to the church and displayed all that had been produced during the day. Icons were displayed between candles on window ledges; paintings were pegged to strings along the side walls; prayer doves were strung across the main aisle; collage banners hung from pillars; wood and clay models appeared in every corner available; the altar frontal was fixed to the temporary nave altar. The graffiti board had been in church since the morning and people had continued to add to it.

The eucharist that ended the day was simple and short and lasted for about forty minutes. People sat in pews, or on the floor round the altar, or on the chancel steps as they felt comfortable. Any sentences and prefaces included in the service were those set for Pentecost in *The Alternative Service Book 1980*, or *Patterns for Worship*.

The music chosen for the eucharist had been used in the music groups, so most people had either sung it or heard it being sung during the day. All the hymns except the communion hymn were accompanied by children with percussion instruments or the streamers that they had made. A fanfare was produced by the instrumental group. The reading of Acts 2 was danced by the dance group. The sermon was very short and consisted of two or three people reading slowly aloud the words and images of Pentecost that had been put on the graffiti board as the day progressed. This was followed by a short silence. The icons and the prayer doves were displayed in such a way that everyone could see some of them, so there was a visual focal point for the intercessions. These intercessions were impromptu, under the leadership of two adults, with individuals praying from their seats.

At the end of the eucharist, to the hymn 'One more step', the cake made by the cooking group was processed round the church and out to the hall with everyone following. When everyone was in the hall, the candles on the cake were lit and 'Happy birthday' was sung to the church. The cake was then cut, shared and eaten before the day finally ended and the clearing up began.

How: afterwards

Most of what had been produced in the activity groups was taken home by participants. Some of it found its way into local churches for display on the following Sunday, Pentecost. More adventurous groups attempted to present to their home congregations something of what had happened on this day by using the dance, the prayers, the icons, the paintings and the prayers in their own services.

Evaluation

Over a cup of tea everyone was invited to complete a simple evaluation form, giving different parts of the day a score of 1 to 4 (1 for disappointing, 4 for very good) and leaving room for optional comments.

The aims of this deanery all age day were to give parishes an experience of working and being together, and to give people more confidence to organise and to run an all age event in their own parish. The planning group held a review meeting to look at the evaluation comments from the day and to make their own assessment of how the event had gone.

About ninety people came to the day, representing about half of the total of thirty Anglican churches in the deanery. The day was definitely an all age day, the youngest person being about two years old, the oldest well over seventy-five. All age does not mean that all ages have to be mixed up all the time; it is sometimes appropriate for similar age groups to work together. For example, the icon activity became an older group and worked well as such. All age is about an open, accepting attitude to others; it means looking for opportunities to do things together, while recognising that this may not always be desirable or sensible. The most difficult group to integrate on this day was the twelve to fourteen age group, who wanted to remain together all the time and who found it hard to settle on one activity for any length of time.

The planning group was mainly pleased with the activities. It was considered that the strength of many activities was not the finished products, but the conversation and discussions that took place between people who would not normally learn from or listen to each other. Busy hands had broken down verbal barriers. In terms of variety, there was plenty from which the adults and children could select, but they felt that the needs of the twelve to fourteen age group could have been addressed more specifically. Better involvement of this age group at the planning stages of the day might have helped.

The idea behind using a not-very-convenient church building met with great approval, and it put a similar day within the reach of people with similarly limited buildings.

Although there has not been a rush to repeat the event in many other parishes in the deanery, some have tried it for themselves. More importantly there seems to be evidence that the skills used or learnt at this day have been utilised in the churches, the Sunday schools, the holiday projects and the worship of the deanery. The aim of increasing confidence appears to have been, at least partially, successful.

Resources

Songs

One more step along the world I go (*Come and Praise* 47)

Bible

Acts 2:1–13 (Pentecost)

Books

Children in the Way, London, Church House Publishing, 1988
Patterns for Worship, London, Church House Publishing, 1995
The Alternative Service Book, London, SPCK, 1980.

5 TEDDY'S PENTECOST

Betty Pedley

Who

To cater for the many young families in our church we have a Parents and Tots group. People always know when that group is meeting because of the confusion of prams and buggies crowding the outer hall. This group is popular with both adults and the children aged from birth to four years. Each week toys are unpacked and gleefully rediscovered by the expectant children, playmats are unrolled and the fun begins. Parents join in many of the games and activities but also have a chance to chat with each other, seek each other's advice and opinion and generally discuss the events of the past week over a cup of coffee. There are not many occasions in the week when such a large group of people are waiting to come into the church building with such expectancy and enthusiasm.

Why

We wished to share this enthusiasm with the rest of the congregation and to involve the children in our regular worship. We decided to bring to one of our communion services the results of our work and play.

When

We chose Pentecost Sunday as a good day for celebration, one which would inspire many activities appropriate for both play and worship. We decided that the four weeks leading up to Pentecost would follow our established pattern but that we would keep the results of our activities for display in the service.

How: teddy

To begin our preparation for Pentecost, we read to the children the adventures of Teddy Horsley in *The Windy Day*. Teddy Horsley is an important part of our activities each week. He is a central character in a collection of 16 books (see Resources) which cover a range of bible teaching such as forgiveness and thankfulness, as well as exploration of the seasons of the church's year: Christmas, Epiphany, Easter and Pentecost.

Many of the parents who bring their children to our Parents and Tots group have no faith commitment or other church connection and the introduction of explicit bible-based activities into our group would be very threatening. By using Teddy Horsley's explorations and discoveries as the basis of our activities, both children and adults are introduced to bible concepts. As Teddy is drawn into the daily conversations and experiences of the household, spiritual concepts are developed.

Over the years, Teddy Horsley has become a loved and accepted member of our group. The group has its own large teddy bear with special clothes to make him look just like his picture in the books. Children take it in turns to care for our Teddy Horsley, to talk to him and to involve him in their play. Every week Teddy shares a story or an experience and the children frequently ask him, 'What's your story about today?'

Many children have their own Teddy Horsleys. Parents and grandparents have been coerced into sewing or knitting a wardrobe of clothes for them. Once a child has his or her own Teddy Horsley, that child can share much from life's experiences with the bear, for teddies are always there to be talked to. They are discreet, tactful, attentive and sympathetic.

How: *The Windy Day*

The Windy Day is the story of Teddy Horsley's discovery of the presence and nature of the Holy Spirit. Teddy learns that though he cannot see, touch or hear the wind, he can see the effect of the wind as it turns washing inside out; he can feel the effect of the wind as it tugs his kite into the sky; he can hear the movement of the wind as it rattles dustbin lids. So too with the Holy Spirit. Teddy Horsley can see the Holy Spirit making people smile and dance; he can feel the Holy Spirit making him safe and loved; he can hear the Holy Spirit making people sing and laugh. Teddy Horsley knows that just as the wind is there, all around him, so too is the Holy Spirit.

This book became the focus of all our Pentecost preparations. As Teddy Horsley experienced the wind, so too our children were given experiences of the wind. They sang and danced, played and drew, and celebrated God's gift of the wind and God's gift of the Holy Spirit.

The learning continued at home as families obtained their own copies of *The Windy Day* and explored them together. Many parents find it hard to talk with their children about the things of God, especially when they are unsure and insecure in such areas themselves. However, reading a Teddy Horsley book together after sharing activities in the group makes it easier for adults and children to grow and explore these aspects of the Christian faith together.

How: activities

To teach the children about the Holy Spirit and to prepare for our Pentecost service, we provided a range of activities for the children in the four weeks leading up to Pentecost. Not every child chose to engage in every activity. We allowed the children to choose for themselves the things they wished to do. Some activities were offered on several occasions so that children who had missed out one week could take part at another time.

Story

The Windy Day was of course our central story and our starting point. Parents and children gathered around together to
enjoy Teddy Horsley's experiences. Children love repetition
and frequently ask for their favourite stories time and again.
By the second week the children were encouraged to join in
with the words, using the pictures as a prompt. By the fourth
week the repeated reading of the story and the repeated pattern
of words within the story had helped many of the children to
learn it by heart. They delighted in telling Teddy's adventures
along with the reader.

Music and dance

Music is an important means of exploration and expression for
children. We sang songs about the wind and played home-
made instruments. We discovered our own wind sounds on
instruments and with our mouths. We learnt the song 'Wind,
wind blow on me' and practised it with instruments.

We created a wind dance where the children were trees with
arms for branches. The children held streamers in each hand.
While a guitarist strummed chords, a drum beat indicated the
noise of a gentle breeze which became louder as the wind got
stronger. After a crescendo the wind quietened to a gentle
breeze again.

Poetry

We read poems about windy weather. We stamped around the
room in time to the poem's rhythm. We moved our arms and
legs as though blown by the poem's wind.

Boats

We folded paper boats and made small models. We provided
plastic boats and wooden boats. These were sailed outside in
a water-filled paddling pool. We used our breath to blow them
over the water. We experimented with different wind effects.
After a rainy day, some of the boats were sailed in puddles.

Kites and balloons

We made and decorated kites. We blew up balloons and drew pictures on them. We took them outside to play. We tied the strings of the balloons to the children's wrists so the children could watch the balloons blow in the wind but would not be distressed by losing them. We released a few balloons when the wind was at its height and watched them tossed over the trees. We watched our kites with delight as some of them soared high into the sky.

Finger puppets

Children enjoy making and playing with puppets. We made simple finger puppets from felt. The base shapes had been cut and glued before the session. The children glued on Teddy's ears and face and clothes. Although all the finger puppets looked different, every child remembered to give Teddy his scarf.

Edible treats

The children always expect something special to eat at the group. Sometimes we prepare our own food and sometimes we provide teddy shaped biscuits. When the children made kites, we also gave them the opportunity to make kite sandwiches. We cut bread to diamond shapes and let the children butter it and decorate it with hundreds and thousands. We added a liquorice tail. When the children made boats, we rolled out biscuit mixture and cut out simple boat shapes and baked them. Later we decorated them with icing.

Mobiles

Mobiles for bedrooms are popular and easy to make. We provided cut-out shapes of boats and balloons and kites. The children decorated these ready to be tied to metal coathangers along with brightly coloured streamers to move in any breeze.

Washing line

Older children prepared a washing line and hung from it the words of John 3:8, 'The wind blows wherever it wishes; you hear the sound it makes, but you do not know where it comes from or where it is going'. These words were written on pieces of paper cut to the shape of items of washing.

Some members of our group could speak other languages and translated this verse for us in preparation for our service, to read it all together in as many languages as possible.

Pictures

We provided a variety of pictorial activities to explore Teddy Horsley's experiences: dot-to-dots for the children to join, mazes to follow Teddy's adventures, pictures to colour, paint or cover with coloured paper, balloon pictures made from potato stamps and paint, and collages of boats at sea and kites tossed by the wind. Some of these pictures were taken home for bedroom or kitchen walls but some were kept for later display in the church.

Free play

As children enjoy creating their own activities, we provided a variety of toys and activities for them, with suggestions of ways they could be used but allowing the children their own creativity to develop ideas. We provided a sand tray, construction toys, dress ups and playdough. The children sifted sand through their fingers, constructed Teddy Horsley's house, dressed up as Teddy ready for windy weather, shaped playdough as boats and balloons and kites, and played in many other ways.

How: the service

The service took the following form.

Welcome
Song, This is the day

Greeting
Confession
Collect for purity
Collect for Pentecost
The Windy Day part 1
Wind dance and reflection
Psalm 104
Acts 2:1-21
Song, Wind, wind, blow on me
John 3:8
Silence
Song, Spirit of the living God
The Windy Day part 2
Red streamers handed to congregation
Song, All over the world
Creed
Intercession
Peace
Offertory hymn, Spirit of God, as strong as the wind
Eucharistic prayer
Lord's prayer
Communion
Hymn, Come down O love divine
Blessing and dismissal

By the time of Pentecost the children were ready to take part in the service. They had experienced the wind in a variety of forms, they had practised their song and their dance of the wind, they knew the story of *The Windy Day*, and they had provided a variety of artwork to be displayed in the church.

With the help of parents and children, pictures were displayed in the entrance hall, the church was decorated with balloons and streamers, and the bible verse washing line was strung near an open window so it could be blown by the wind. As older children in the church had also been preparing for this service, their artwork was displayed along with that of the pre-schoolers.

People had been invited to come to the Pentecost service early in order to join the children in flying kites outside. Then as the start to the service itself the entire congregation walked around the perimeter of the church singing and carrying balloons and streamers.

The story *The Windy Day* was read in two parts. The first part tells of the effect of the wind while the second part tells of the effect of the Holy Spirit in the lives of people and in their worship. The story was read with story boards, large pictures copied from the book with accompanying captions. Where possible, real objects, such as dustbin lids, were displayed.

During the wind dance, the pre-school children were joined by older children who had also practised the dance. As they watched, the congregation was asked to reflect on the presence and action of the wind.

The Gospel reading was the single verse from John 3:8. It was first proclaimed in English, then separately in other languages. To give the effect of the babble of the first Pentecost, these proclamations were followed by the verse in all languages at once.

As part of the offertory, examples of the children's work were also offered.

Evaluation

This was truly an all age service with the gifts and talents of different age groups contributing to the qualities of the whole in ways which no narrow age-band of people could have created or experienced.

The involvement of the pre-school children and their parents in preparation gave them an interest in the festival of Pentecost and in the service itself. Many of the families who came along did so as a result of being involved in preparation. They would not have come to join in the celebration if they had not become involved in this way through their mid-week group.

The young children had a very real part to play in the service in ways which helped to focus their attention and also to help them to develop a sense of belonging. It helped adults to recognise and accept these young children as part of the whole church too. It was good for the very young children to be joined by the older children who had also been involved in their own preparation with artwork, the dance and the songs.

For older members of the congregation this was an experience of the family of the church celebrating its birthday together. The life and excitement of the children, the babble of the language, the colour of the streamers, the simplicity of the message (John 3:8) combined to make this Pentecost one to remember.

I was so thrilled by the quality of the preparation and the interest and enquiry which it aroused, it made me recognise the potential of the Teddy Horsley stories for exploring religious truths with young children and their families. It was from this that the idea of *Ready, Teddy, God!* was born. This is a resource book to help young children to explore their faith through experiential learning in ways which can lead to deeper involvement in the Christian faith and in the worship of the church.

Resources

Songs

All over the world, the Spirit is moving (*Mission Praise* 293)
Come down, O love divine (*Hymns Ancient and Modern New Standard* 156)
Spirit of God, as strong as the wind (*Come and Praise* 63)
Spirit of the living God, fall afresh on me (*Sound of Living Waters* 29)
This is the day (*Sound of Living Waters* 13)
Wind, wind, blow on me (*Fresh Sounds* 52)

Bible

Psalm 104
Acts 2:1–2
John 3:8

Books

Leslie J Francis, Nicola M Slee and Betty Pedley, *Ready, Teddy, God!*, Birmingham, NCEC, 1997

The *Teddy Horsley* series, written by Leslie J Francis and Nicola M Slee and illustrated by Laura Cooper, is published by the National Christian Education Council. Individual titles include:

The Windy Day: Teddy Horsley and the Holy Spirit
The Picnic: Teddy Horsley goes to communion
The Song: Teddy Horsley and the Song of Creation
The Sunny Morning: Teddy Horsley celebrates the new life of Easter
Lights: Teddy Horsley celebrates Christmas
The Present: Teddy Horsley meets the wise men
Good Morning: Teddy Horsley learns to be thankful
Do and Tell: Teddy Horsley talks to God
Explorer: Teddy Horsley wonders at God's handiwork
Music Makers: Teddy and Betsy make music
The Grumpy Day: Teddy Horsley learns about forgiveness
Night Time: Teddy Horsley feels safe at night
Neighbours: Betsy Bear helps her neighbours
The Walk: Betsy Bear senses God's care
Water: Teddy Horsley and baptism
Autumn: Betsy Bear learns about death

Some of the Teddy Horsley stories are also available in large format collections:

Out and About with Teddy Horsley
A Day with Teddy Horsley

6 CARNIVAL TIME

Anne Faulkner

Why

One of the high points of the year on the Britwell estate for the last 30 years has been the carnival. The estate has 17,000 inhabitants of all ages, three large schools, a complete range of guiding and scouting groups and many community organisations, all of whom have some part in the carnival. By local tradition, every year the carnival starts with a service in the parish church of St George on the Sunday evening, continues with events in the community every evening for the next week, building up to the carnival procession and the carnival dance on the following Saturday.

Because of the high level of interest in the carnival from many individuals and organisations in the community, it is important for this service to be a good experience. Of the people who have been involved in the carnival for 30 years, no one is very sure why it begins with a service in the church, but they believe it is for celebration and thanksgiving. The carnival service is certainly one of the few occasions in the year when significant numbers from the local community attend church other than for baptisms, weddings and funerals. A large proportion of the regular congregation also attends.

The following description of a recent carnival service is fairly typical of the services in the last few years.

Where

The carnival service is held in the parish church of St George, a 1960s modern building with a good open space and car park in front. This open space is important as people choose to gather together before going inside. The inside of the building is spacious with a wide centre aisle which invites movement round the church. The chairs are movable and generally visibility is good.

When

The carnival service is held every year. The date is set by the carnival committee, then checked out with the vicar. This year it was planned for the second Sunday in June at 6.30, to last about 50 minutes so that everyone would be free to leave before 7.30.

How: planning

Members of the carnival committee were strongly encouraged to be involved in the planning of the service but they declined with the words 'The church does it very nicely thank you'. This particular year there was no special theme for the carnival but the District Church Council decided on the theme of 'the streets of the estate' for the decorations in the church building.

The church worship committee discussed ways of encouraging people to produce decorations for the church, and ways to help people feel involved in the service. They also discussed the music and the production of service sheets. The congregation generally felt pleased about the carnival service and wanted to talk about it, to publicise it and to actively support it.

How: publicity

Publicity was the dual responsibility of the carnival committee and the church members. As is its usual practice, the carnival committee produced a carnival week programme of all carnival events, which was distributed to every house in the neighbourhood. Details of the service appeared in the programme, together with an invitation from the vicar for all to attend.

The church worship committee produced posters for shops, houses, schools and halls on the estate. These posters were home produced on the photocopier to keep the expenses as low as possible. The layout was simple, designed to be coloured by children or adults to make the posters more conspicuous and eye catching.

The most effective publicity was by word of mouth. Teachers and leaders told children, children told their families, individuals told other individuals and so the news spread.

How: decorations

Schools and children's organisations were asked in advance to produce paintings, collages, pictures or photographs to be displayed in church. The children of the church, the Sunday school and Weeny Worship (the midweek worship for under fives) were encouraged to make posters and banners. These were all to show streets on the estate, activity in the streets or gardens or anything that depicted the actual street names.

A wide range of material was produced: fabric collages, large pictures made by groups of people, small pictures from individuals, large wall hangings and colourful paintings. Several groups produced clever interpretations of street names: Wordsworth Road was shown as 'a host of golden daffodils', Fosters Path as a large glass of beer, and Monksfield Way quite literally as a monk standing in a green field. Members of the church youth group helped to display all this material.

How: rehearsals

The carnival committee produced two readers for the service. Neither person had read in church before, and one was the junior carnival queen who was only 10 years old. On the Friday before the service both readers came to church to rehearse, together with friends to support and encourage them. This rehearsal was taken by the vicar.

How: costumes

Those attending the carnival service were encouraged to dress up. Some extravert individuals really enjoyed this, wearing silly hats, masks, or even full costumes. Others preferred less flamboyant costumes, women choosing long skirts, shawls and hats, and men choosing eye catching ties and waistcoats. The Brownies worked together to be a Chinese dragon, about 20 of them underneath as the legs with a long fabric covering to make the body. It was very effective as it snaked about the car park before the service; never has a dragon giggled so much. The Guides came dressed as St Trinians school girls, the Cub Scouts as pirates, younger girls wore bridesmaids' dresses, other children and adults came as clowns.

The church youth group and some adult members of the congregation wore the parish teeshirts, which are red with a yellow St George and the dragon. They sat in the choir stalls to give a lead to the singing.

How: the service

The service took the following form.

    Hymn, Give me oil in my lamp
    Welcome
    Preparation for worship
    Gloria/hymn
    Carnival collect
    Reading, 2 Samuel 6:12–19
    Hymn, Come and praise the Lord
    Reading, Matthew 11:16–19
    Address
    Prayers
    Peace
    Hymn, All people that on earth do dwell

Collection for the carnival charity
Blessing
Hymn, One more step along the world I go

The service was very loosely based on the ministry of the word from the rite A communion service, *The Alternative Service Book 1980*. This is the main service at St George's every Sunday morning, so anyone at the carnival service who decided to come on a Sunday morning would find the shape of the worship familiar.

The music for the service was provided by an electronic keyboard for some items and by a piano for others. In other years the organ has also been used, and on one occasion the steel band from the local school helped out. The majority of people who came to this service were not used to being in church, knew almost no hymns and were very shy about singing in a public place. This meant that the accompaniment to the hymns needed to stress the melody fairly forcefully and confidently to make it easy for people to join in.

The hymns were chosen to include some traditional favourites, modern favourites including those the children had learned at local schools, and songs with words specially written for this service based on popular secular tunes that most would know. Clapping, percussion instruments, jigging about, swaying and stamping feet were all encouraged to accompany the hymns.

Opening hymn

During the opening song, the Brownies' dragon led the procession into the church, coiling its way all round the building and coming to rest in specially reserved seats. The two local groups of majorettes came next, parading around the church with batons twirling. They were followed by members of the carnival court and officials. The court consisted of a junior and a senior carnival queen, together with attending princesses, all dressed appropriately in long dresses, tiaras and velvet cloaks. The officials in the procession were the president and the chairman of the carnival. The vicar followed them wearing a special stole made for the event with a design depicting Teddy Horsley holding large multi coloured bunches of balloons.

Welcome

Everyone was invited to sit down after the hymn. Various groups known to be present in church were welcomed by name and asked to respond by waving or standing up and making a bow. Organisations were named, schools were referred to and people known to be visiting from other areas or places were mentioned. One family had some Australian relatives staying with them and they were welcomed; so was another person known to be on holiday from Holland. This welcome was done with much cheering and waving within the spirit of carnival and celebration.

Preparation for worship

This was a very simple penitential act with a short invitation to remember the past, to pause for a moment and to repeat 'Lord have mercy, Christ have mercy, Lord have mercy'. The words were written on the service sheet for those who were not familiar with them. This was followed by the words of absolution.

Gloria

The specially written gloria (see Appendix) was sung to the tune of 'Early one morning'. Most people knew the tune and found it easy to sing.

Carnival collect

The carnival was then proclaimed using as a collect the poem 'Come Holy Harlequin' by Sidney Carter.

Readings

The two carnival queens read 2 Samuel 6:12-19 and Matthew 11:16-19. Both readings introduced the theme of dancing. Between these readings was a hymn.

Hymn

The hymn after the first reading is an example of a well known tune, 'Knees up Mother Brown', being used with special words. This hymn was successful as it made people smile, feel at ease and helped them to join in with gusto. The Guides, all standing in the congregation in a long row, spontaneously danced in time to the music.

Address

In place of a sermon, the vicar gave a short talk involving young people to help him in the front, and encouraging everyone to answer questions and to answer him back. In the past, visitors have been invited to give the address but it has generally been agreed that people like to hear their vicar whom they know, who knows them, who can strike the right tone, make them laugh, say something they can understand and give them something to go away and think about if they want to.

Prayers

Members of the congregation who were used to leading intercessions on a Sunday morning led short and simple prayers of thanksgiving and intercession. Thanks was given for those who work hard to sustain the life of the local community, for the carnival, and for the joy of celebration. Intercession was made for the events of the coming carnival week, for the life of the community, for local needs and local named people who were ill or absent. The Lord's prayer was said and a carnival prayer used (see Appendix).

Peace

An invitation was given for all to exchange the peace. Normally on a Sunday morning the congregation moves around the church to exchange the peace, but with such a crowd of people this was not possible at the carnival service. Regular members of the congregation led the shaking of hands and the hugs, and it was not long before everyone joined in.

The peace took some few minutes to complete as people greeted each other and complimented each other on fancy dress costumes.

Collection hymn

By contrast to others in this service, this hymn was a traditional one, 'All people that on earth do dwell'. It was known to most of the older people and was vaguely familiar to younger people who had heard it on television.

Every year the carnival committee selects a local charity to receive all money that is donated. This year it was the kidney unit at the local hospital and the church collection was given entirely to this cause. The church kept nothing for the expenses as the service is considered an important part of its outreach.

Final hymn

'One more step along the world I go' is a St George's special. It is a firm favourite, especially with the younger people. It was sung several times, each time getting louder. Those wanting to do so followed the Brownies' dragon and the majorettes, singing and stamping all round the church to the car park outside.

During the hymn others made their way to the back of the church and stood chatting and laughing in the summer sunshine. Many people lingered for a chat and photographs and it was well after 8.00 before the church was clear.

Evaluation

It proved to be difficult to get those who attended to say how the service could have been improved. They were generous with their praise and their thanks, and certainly attended in large numbers, as they do every year. The church worship committee made its own evaluation, agreeing that the weakness of the event was the lack of carnival committee involvement in the planning. More encouragement would be given in future years.

The general impression was that everyone enjoyed the old tunes being used as hymns and loved the party atmosphere. A child who regularly attends church on a Sunday morning spoke for many when she said, 'I wish every Sunday was carnival Sunday'. Perhaps it should be!

Resources

Songs

All people that on earth do dwell (*Hymns Ancient and Modern New Standard* 100)

Give me oil in my lamp keep me burning (*Come and Praise* 43)

One more step along the world I go (*Come and Praise* 47)

Bible

2 Samuel 6:12–19 (David danced before the Lord)
Matthew 11:16–19 (Jesus is accused of celebrating)

Books

The Alternative Service Book 1980, London, SPCK, 1980
Sidney Carter, *Green Print for Song*, London, Galliard, 1974
Leslie J Francis and Nicola M Slee, *The Windy Day: Teddy Horsley and the Holy Spirit*, Birmingham, NCEC, 1983

Appendix

Gloria (to the tune of 'Early one morning')

Glory to ou-our God, the one God in the hi-ighest,
And peace on ea-earth to all people of good will,
Oh how we worship you,
Oh how we tha-ank you,
We-ee praise your glo-ory our great and heavenly king.

As our cre-a-ator you a-are the begi-inning,
Father and Mo-other of all things that have been.
Oh how we worship you,
Oh how we tha-ank you,
We-ee praise your glo-ory our hea-ea-eav'nly king.

Lord Jesus Chri-i-ist, Son of the Heavenly Fa-ather,
– You are our Go-od and our Sacrificial Lamb,
Bearer of this world's sin
Have mercy o-on us
No-ow and for ever hear the pra-ayers that we bring.

You are the holy one, alone our Lord and God most high
With the Holy Spi-irit, our Saviour Jesus Christ,
In God's great glo-ory
In the highest hea-eaven
He-ere on the ea-arth we-ee si-ing ou-out loud.
Amen.

Come and praise the lord (to the tune of 'Knees up Mother
Brown'; © Peter C Faulkner)

Come and praise the Lord,
Come and praise the Lord,
Britwell* people shout and sing:
Jesus, Jesus Christ is King!
If He finds me sinning,
He's died to set me free!
Alleluia! Alleluia!
Blessed forgiven me.

Oh my, what a holy song!
What a holy song! What a holy song!
Oh my what a holy song
And in Jesus we'll be holy too!

* The name can be changed to fit many places or 'all you people' could be
sung instead.

Prayer for carnival
Flame dancing Spirit come.
Sweep us off our feet and dance us through our days.
Surprise us with your rhythms.
Dare us to try new steps,
to explore new patterns and partnerships.
Release us from old routines
to swing in abandoned joy and fearful adventures.
And in the intervals, rest us in your still centre.
Amen.

7 INVOLVING SCHOOLS

Martin Warner

Why

The priests and people of St Peter's, Plymouth, were concerned that the two church schools of the parish had become isolated from the life of the generally ageing Sunday morning congregation. A Programme to Schools was planned to present Christianity as part of a balanced religious education syllabus. This programme was to be a service to all schools, including those in the independent sector.

The parish clergy and the governors and teaching staff of the church schools recognised the importance of the spiritual dimension in a balanced religious education syllabus. They also recognised the contributions that could be made by those who worked within the local community, and wished to provide opportunity for people of any age to express their faith.

What

The theme chosen was the diverse nature of Christian vocation. This would include not only distinctive vocations such as the priesthood and the religious life, but also lay Christians who could talk about how their faith related to their work and way of life. The programme was planned to use the church building to teach what Christianity is about.

Although the subject matter of the programme reflected our particular tradition in the Catholic wing of the Church of England, it nevertheless aimed at providing something simple, fairly universal within the Christian tradition as a whole, and factual. The theme of vocation provided objective information and personal testimony which allowed participants to glean information without making credal demands, while opening up the possibility of dialogue for those who wanted it.

Who

The programme in Plymouth was to pupils of primary and secondary school age. Terminology in such cases is always difficult. We chose to use the term 'young people' to include as wide an age group as possible. The word 'child' seemed to have a more limited and specific application, and one which teenagers would have found highly insulting. The New Testament, however, is less nuanced, or perhaps more bold, in its descriptions. The following quotation was in the entrance to both the primary and secondary schools in St Peter's Parish; it neatly sums up the reason for our concern with schools:

Whoever welcomes one little child like this in my name welcomes me.

The programme team was drawn from within the parish and further afield, the objective and independent viewpoint of people from outside being a valuable contribution to the assessment of the programme and our future work. The team consisted of a range of people, young and old, clergy, laity and religious. Ordinands had a great deal to offer, being students themselves, and generally nearer the age range of those we were targeting. In fact their youthfulness was one of the greatest assets, since it challenged the impression that everyone in church was elderly.

Collaboration between the parish and a variety of religious education departments was found to be particularly helpful for teachers. This became the task of the parish priest responsible for day to day work in the church aided schools. During the programme, contact with non-denominational state maintained schools provided the parish with an extended opportunity to meet young people from the locality and to use our most valuable teaching resource, the church building, in a wider context.

Where

St Peter's, Plymouth, is a disadvantaged inner-city parish in a predominantly white British area of England.

While it must be true that the church is most authentically people and not buildings, it should also be true that the church building makes some significant statement about the people who use it. Therefore the programme chose to use the church building to teach about Christianity. In this way the building became a significant meeting place. First, it was where those with no Christian experience met with different types of Christians. Second, it was the place where the experience of worship could be met, but with the sensitivities of non-Christians respected and guarded.

When

The end of term can be a fraught time for weary teaching staff in any school, but we found that it was also the moment when an adjustment to the timetable was possible, even desirable. All the local schools agreed that the end of summer term would be the best time for this event.

The programme lasted for a school week, culminating outside school time with the usual Sunday morning worship. Other activities outside the school timetable were also important, providing an opportunity for young people to meet informally and follow up new discoveries.

How: planning

Because of the diverse nature of the theme of vocation, lay involvement was fundamental in planning. The parish as a whole felt a clear commitment to the enterprise and laity were involved in all stages in such a way that they were able to 'own' the programme.

We began planning very early on, in order to include other schools as well as the church ones, and in order to make maximum use of the opportunity. We had begun planning by the end of the academic year before the programme took place.

In order to introduce the idea to schools other than our own, it was important to provide clear evidence of the usefulness of the programme, particularly for the religious education department, and therefore to know something about the syllabus each school used. We also needed to show the event as exciting, in order to stimulate interest for participation. When offering a draft timetable to schools we found it helpful to maintain a balance between structured events available to everyone and independent events which could be adapted to any school timetable or other grouping (for example, nursery or parent and toddler group).

Balance was similarly needed in the range of activities on offer, ensuring that events in school time were matched by instructive but enjoyable events after school. Events for young people were matched by all age events which included church and non-church people, providing laity with an opportunity to take their part in the programme.

It was vital that during the period of the programme, people in the team should be available for this activity alone and no other. Early planning was necessary because of the time demands made on those who would take part. Religious communities, especially, were snowed under with requests and so needed advance warning. But of equal importance was the distinctive lay vocation. It was quite difficult to find laity who were available for the whole week, particularly since committed and articulate lay folk already have so many demands on their time. But the impact of lay Christians who could talk about how their faith related to their work and way of life was very powerful. In most cases their participation was possible because people took time off from their working day. Among the most memorable were a chef who spoke about being a shop steward in his union, and a probation officer who spoke about her work with ex-offenders.

In addition to the programme team and members of the congregation, we drew heavily on the skills of people who came in as consultants, perhaps for one or two sessions. Many different leaders, including musicians, dramatists and games players, all helped with different aspects of the programme.

Care for the programme team was vital. This provided yet another opportunity for laity to make an invaluable contribution. We needed to ensure that team members were comfortable in the places where they were staying and able to come and go as necessary, with no worries about transport. Meal times were designed to provide either a time of escape from exposure to an audience, or a social event which was also work. Care of the programme team had to include time for them to be alone, to plan, to relax and to pray.

How: publicity

We discovered that schools had their own excellent system of communication. They needed from us publicity material which was simple, attractive and of a high standard. Posters and hand outs were useful, as were stickers, although the latter were sometimes used a little indiscriminately. The most important aspect was being written in to the school timetable, and that often took a lot of negotiation and co-ordination.

How: programme

The programme is outlined below. Further details of some events are given in the next section.

Sunday

Programme team arrives
Planning session
Parish party: 'getting to know you'

Monday

School assemblies
Workshop: priesthood (11.00–12.00)*

Mass and picnic lunch (12.15)*
School visits and presentations
Planning evening

Tuesday

School assemblies or presentations
Workshop: religious (11.00–12.00)*
Mass and packed lunch (12.15)*
School visits and presentations
Planning session
Video evening

Wednesday

School assemblies or presentation
Workshop: laity (11.00–12.00)*
Mass and packed lunch (12.15)*
School visits and presentations
Games evening

Thursday

Outing, particularly for the children and parents from the
   church school
Evening mass and disco

Friday

School assemblies
School visits and presentations
Review of the programme
Drama*

Saturday

Day off for programme team
Drama*

Sunday

Parish mass and barbecue

* These items all took place in the church. We were fortunate in having a
building which could be used in a variety of ways. This was a distinct
advantage, since it brought people across the threshold, often for the first
time, and perhaps afforded them the only non-threatening experience of
this kind of building they had ever had.

How: events

Planning sessions

An opportunity for the programme team to be alone to plan
their activities was a vital part of the daily timetable. It also
provided support during a pressurised week, and an outlet for
frustrations. The team had clear instructions about what was
expected of them, where they were going each day, what was
likely to happen and whom they would meet. They also had to
be ready to think on their feet and adapt easily to a constantly
changing situation.

Workshops

Workshops in church provided a setting for the presentations
on vocation. The building offered visual aids, some of which
stimulated discussion beyond the prescribed topic. It was
important to ensure that the pupils felt at home in what was to
some of them a very strange building. We were fortunate in
being able to adapt the building quite easily to meet their
needs.

Schools visits and presentations

Presentations in schools was the part of the programme most
closely geared towards a particular part of the curriculum. In
some cases it was possible to fit these in with an existing religious education lesson; in other cases special arrangements
were made. This opportunity demanded that the presentation

was of a high standard, factual, brief, and the equipment used (for example, video, cassette tapes) had to be easy to carry and operate.

Video evening

The video evening was an opportunity to provide the programme team with an enjoyable event to which those who wished to be involved could be invited. It need not have been a specifically Christian film. (*Ben Hur* provided some unexpected moments of amusement!) The value was in meeting outside school time.

Games evening

The games evening was partly directed towards younger children but offered something for quite a wide age range. It took place in church because it was based on the principle that play (even in a fairly sophisticated form) and learning are two aspects of the same experience. The games were specifically designed to use the church building, without any lack of reverence, and involved drama, a treasure hunt and a mime.

Outing

The outing took the form of a children's outing to the cathedral. Parents were invited, many of them not regular church people. This gave the school something specific to work towards within the programme, and prolonged access to the programme team. It proved to be one of the most memorable events of the week, and among the happiest.

Evening mass and disco

The evening mass took place in the same hall as the disco. It attracted a lot of younger children and their parents. The mass was integrated into the evening as part of the celebration, and drew on the party mood. It was a way of pointing to the Christian vocation of joy, not always easily perceived by young people in the church.

Drama

The drama was devised and produced by drama students, using religious education classes from local schools. It provided an opportunity for older pupils to prepare for the programme and give expression to their own understanding of the question of faith in their lives. It was not an explicitly Christian play, but the theme of quest was seen as a positive response to the programme theme.

Parish mass and barbecue

Many of the young people who were involved in programme activities were invited to the parish mass and barbecue, as were their parents. Some expressed interest; a few actually came. That was not the measure of success. The important thing for the parish was that they had done something and during the course of the week a lot of young people had been inside the church building. The barbecue was a celebration of that achievement and a thank you to the team and all the lay folk who had made it possible.

Evaluation

The review at the end of the week was very important; out of it came specific ideas for the next stages of development of this work in the parish.

This programme brought home to us the reality of young people's perceptions about Christianity. Very often Christianity was seen by them as something novel, esoteric and unrelated to their experience. We might have expected similar comments to be made by white British children about Islam or Hinduism. But we began to see the extent to which we had yet to recognise fully, and tackle, the gulf of perception and experience which exists between the church and those that are outside that sometimes narrowly defined circle. The experience of this kind of activity, and participation in it, encouraged us to find ways of bridging that gulf. It helped us to put work with young people high on the list of priorities.

The involvement of laity at all stages of the programme resulted in their willingness to undertake ongoing work with young people in the future.

It is impossible and undesirable to try to estimate the success of this programme in St Peter's parish. Young people will not be bought or bribed to come to church by a week's activities, no matter how enjoyable they were. But we were convinced that there would be lasting value in trying to show that Christians are not only anxious to share their faith and their buildings; they are also willing to adapt themselves to whatever is necessary for that to happen. Perhaps the greatest transformation that came out of the programme was in the perceptions of the congregation. But these perceptions and the contacts with young people which had been made during the programme needed to be nurtured and encouraged, time and attention lavished upon them, and this could only be something that the priest and the people shared together.

In a similar way, the contact with schools, especially with teaching staff, needed to be nurtured. The programme described here demonstrated that the church and its personnel was a resource which could be used at any time. Co-operation brought respect for different disciplines and a recognition of benefit to the pupil. But staff change, clergy move, resources become outmoded. In Plymouth the needs of schools, even a year after the programme, had moved on, and while some contacts were lost, others developed.

8 SAINT JAMES

Brian R Tubbs

Why

Saint James is the patronal saint of St James, Exeter. Saint James' day fell on a Saturday and we wanted a day in which the whole congregation could celebrate and at the same time learn about Saint James. We wanted to work together, have fun together, share with each other, and at the end of the day bring everything together in celebrating the mass.

Where

The church of St James is a modern building with chairs that can be moved, rather than fixed pews. Adjoining the church is a large hall with kitchen facilities.

When

We came together for a Saturday. The day began at 11.00 with an act of worship, followed by the first activity session. Lunch was at 1.00, with everyone bringing their own food, though drinks were provided. A second activity session was held in the afternoon and the day culminated in the sung mass at 4.00.

How: publicity

Publicity was given through the parish magazine and the weekly news sheet. We have a large Sunday school and also have close links with the uniformed organisations, and invitations were sent out to the children to join us. Publicity made it clear that the day was an all age event. Lists were put at the back of the church for three or four weeks before the event, asking people to sign up for three activities. Although each person only took part in two activities, this third choice enabled us to move people around when a particular activity was oversubscribed.

How: planning

Members of the congregation were approached and asked if they would be prepared to lead certain activities. Each leader found and prepared his or her own materials, with the use of books from the parish library. Obviously because of the different demands, some activities were only run once whereas others had both a morning and afternoon session. By approaching the congregation we were able to run the following activities: drama, researching the life of Saint James, intercessions, vestment and altar frontals, stained glass windows, candles, bread, icons, banners, music and sermon.

Using the lists that people had signed, we were able to give the leaders an idea of numbers. It was at this point that decisions were made as to which activities would run twice and which would only run once. All activities included both adults and children, as it was felt it would be beneficial for all to work together.

How: programme

11.00 Act of worship
11.30 Morning activities
 1.00 Lunch break
 2.00 Afternoon activities
 3.30 Preparation for mass
 4.00 Mass

The act of worship was held in the church. At the end, people were told which activity they would be joining. Individuals who had not signed up before went to the activity of their choice as far as was possible.

All work stopped at 1.00 to enable us to eat our packed lunches together in the church hall. Drinks were provided. As the children finished eating, they went outside in the garden for games before the afternoon activities.

How: morning activities

Intercessions

This group met just once in the morning. The brief was 'to prepare in an imaginative way the intercessions for the sung mass'. The group worked out their own intercessions using a variety of materials and books. Each section of the intercessions was allocated to a different person so that as many people as possible were involved.

Vestments

In order to make the vestments that the priest wore for the mass, this group used books and catalogues to get ideas. They made sure they incorporated Saint James into their designs. They started with a large piece of material and cut, stuck, sewed and painted until the finished product was produced.

Stained glass windows

This activity was run both morning and afternoon. Each person was given a picture either of Saint James or something else relevant. The pictures had a border of about 5 cm. Then two frames were cut for each picture from black sugar paper. Each frame was approximately 6 cm wide. The pictures were coloured with felt tip pens, then coated with cooking oil, taking care not to get any oil on the border. (Cooking oil produces a translucent effect. Only a small amount should be used and any excess should be wiped away with kitchen paper.) The pictures were then mounted in the sugar paper frames.

Candle making

This activity was run just once in the morning. The equipment for making the candles was purchased from the local craft shop. Various moulds were used, including scallop shells, which are the emblem of Saint James. Various colours were used and some of the candles ended up multicoloured.

Banners

This activity ran morning and afternoon and produced two entirely different banners. The groups themselves chose the designs from their own thoughts as well as from books.

Sermon

This activity was planned for the morning session as the priest intended to preach the sermon using ideas put forward by the group. The priest needed time between this activity and the mass to work out exactly what he was going to say.

Icons

The person running this activity supplied various sized blocks of wood, to fit a variety of different icons. Each block of wood had a small hole drilled in the back so that it could later be hung on a wall. Pictures were drawn and then mounted onto the wood and varnished. These were fairly easy to do and the children found them great fun. Quite a few spares were made to give to members of the congregation who were unable to attend the day.

How: afternoon activities

Drama

The group chose for themselves the drama to perform. One person read Mark 12:1-12 while the others mimed.

Researching the life of Saint James

This group worked hard, using books and articles about Saint James, so that each person produced a piece of work for a scrap book. Some pieces were written articles while others were drawings or paintings.

Altar frontal

As with the vestment activity of the morning, this group started with a plain piece of material and made the altar frontal. They decided to have it matching the vestments and used material which was cut, stuck, sewed and painted.

Bread

This group kept busy in the kitchen making the bread for the mass. They made two plaited loaves. A word of warning to anyone else who tries this: they made far too much bread, which resulted in the priest spending the next week trying to consume it all from the reserved sacrament!

Music

With the help of a music teacher from the congregation, this group chose the hymns for the mass and also practised playing their instruments to accompany everyone. We were fortunate to have flutes, clarinets, double bass, violins, guitars and various percussion instruments.

How: the mass

At 3.30 everyone got together in the church with all the items prepared for the mass. Chairs were placed in a semi-circle round the altar and each person was given a helium filled balloon which they tied to the back of their chairs. The stained glass windows were displayed round the church; the altar frontal was put on the altar; the candles were either placed on the altar or on small tables at the side, together with the scrap book on the life of Saint James; the icons were displayed around the base of the altar; the banners were placed behind the altar.

Once everything was in place there was a plenary session to give everyone time to practise the hymns that had been chosen. A few of them were new ones, unfamiliar to some of the congregation.

The mass began at 4.00 with the priest resplendent in his new vestments. The music was wonderful and everyone enjoyed the drama. The intercessions proved to be very thought provoking. At the exchange of the peace, each person took a balloon outside and let it go.

Evaluation

The day was attended by people from the ages of 3 up to 96. It was a very successful day and everyone was grateful to have had the time together, and to have learnt so much about Saint James. They appreciated being able to assemble all their efforts into the mass.

Resources

Bible

Mark 12:1-12 (Parable of vineyard)

Books

The Alternative Service Book 1980, London, SPCK, 1980
D Attwater (ed.), *Penguin Dictionary of Saints*, Harmondsworth, Penguin, 1983

9 WALKING THE WAY

Stephen Cottrell

Why

When I became priest-in-charge of a parish for the first time I was shocked to find hardly any young people in church. Like many churches there was a Sunday school and quite a lot of children involved in church life, but almost all of them seemed to lapse at about the time they went to secondary school. I wanted the church to be a place where young people were welcome but I did not know where to begin. I needed to make contact with the teenagers who had lapsed, and I also wanted to find a way of reaching out to the hundreds of teenagers growing up in the parish who knew little or nothing about the Christian faith.

As a curate in south London I had been involved in leading a number of walking pilgrimages to Walsingham in Norfolk. These had been very successful. On one occasion over sixty young people from a number of churches had walked over a hundred miles from north Essex to the north Norfolk coast. These pilgrimages had drawn upon existing youth groups and had sought to encourage young people in their faith. Could the idea of a walking pilgrimage also be a means of reaching those who had no faith and drawing back to the church those who had lapsed?

One of the great themes of the bible is that of *exodus*. The people of God are called to be a people on the move. God invites Moses to lead the people of Israel from slavery in Egypt to the promise of a new beginning. Likewise in the New Testament, the church is called to be a pilgrim people: the Christian life is a new exodus, a journey out of bondage to freedom. If it were possible to gather together a group of young people, would the process of actually making a pilgrimage help them to see that the Christian faith, which they so often seemed to experience as something dry and static, is a way of life, something living and moving forward?

The teenage years are a time of questioning and searching. Young people begin the painful process of leaving the security of home and beginning to discover independence and adulthood. Their bodies start changing and developing. Sexuality is encountered, bringing tremendous joys and heart-rending anxieties. As a child, life did seem stable and secure. As a teenager one is acutely aware that life is a journey. Decisions need to be made. A direction needs to be set.

Going on pilgrimage to a holy place has not only renewed the faith of Christians in every age but it has also helped encourage an awareness that life is a pilgrimage. Life has a beginning and an end. Life has a destination and the route we take through life and who we choose as our companions and our guides is of the utmost significance. From the Christian perspective life is a journey home, the church is a pilgrim people and Jesus, who came to meet us, is our guide along the way.

I am also aware of a basic thrust in all Christian experience which begins with something particular. God is not just an idea. Although we believe God's presence is everywhere, before this can ever begin to be understood we have to experience God somewhere. This, surely, is the meaning of the Incarnation. God becomes known in a particular place and in a particular person. I hoped that a pilgrimage to a particular holy place would give the young people who came an *experience* of the Christian life.

Above all I wanted to make this pilgrimage, with whichever young people I could muster, a demonstration of faith in action. By making a journey together we could show that the church does have a sense of direction and a sense of adventure. Also, by living as a little community, working together and travelling light, we could discover something about being the church on the move. This would not only enrich our lives but should also be great fun!

Where

Canterbury is one of the most important Christian sites in England. It was from here that Augustine began the evangelisation of England, working with the indigenous English church that had been established by previous missionary visits. It is the site of the martyrdom of Thomas Becket. In the crypt is the ancient pilgrim shrine of Our Lady Undercroft. Behind the high altar is the contemporary shrine to twentieth century Christian martyrs. It is the Mother Church of the Anglican Communion.

Conveniently for us, Canterbury is about 150 miles away from our church in Chichester, a perfect distance for a week's pilgrimage. I wanted the walk to be really demanding, not for its own sake but so there would be a real feeling of achievement when we arrived. Canterbury was also a good destination since it is the one pilgrim site many young people have heard of through their school studies of Chaucer.

I also wanted the pilgrimage to be to a place of holiness, somewhere particular. There is something very basic about the desire to visit specific places of significance for our lives. From the earliest times Christians visited the Holy Land, especially those places associated with Jesus. Canterbury has similar significance for the Church of England; it is a holy place.

When

I planned the pilgrimage for the first full week of the school summer holiday. Although this might cut some people out it seemed the best time since we needed a whole week and the weather in England is safest this time of year. You can get rain at any time of course, but I have led similar pilgrimages during Easter holidays and have found times of severe cold.

Since this pilgrimage to Canterbury, I have also led short weekend pilgrimages. You can still cover a fair distance in a weekend, though there is not the same sense of achievement that follows a whole week on the road.

How: publicity

Publicity was the biggest problem. The initial plans, fixing some dates, deciding on a destination, even getting another adult to help me, were made without ever having a single young person to come along!

I felt that, for something as big as this, it was not sufficient to put posters in the local school and hope for the best. The only way I would get people to join me on this pilgrimage was to personally enthuse them with the idea. I drew up a list of all the young people with whom I had contact, restricting my list to teenagers. The total list of about twenty-five names included the one or two teenagers who still occasionally came to church, the lapsed teenagers of churchgoing parents, and a few others whom I had met through my ministry. I then wrote to each of them, inviting them to a barbecue at my house but not mentioning the pilgrimage, and posted the letters. I worked on the assumption that it is still quite rare for most teenagers to receive a letter through the post, and this alone might encourage them to take a bit of notice.

About twelve turned up to the barbecue. There was a good deal of initial embarrassment to be overcome. I had arranged a few games and thought of a few things to do, but they were a mixed bag of mixed ages. Some were meeting me for the first time. It was the first time they had ever been together as a group. However, by the end of the evening, and after embarrassment had subsided, it was a lot better than I could have expected. Also, and amazingly, I had planted the idea of the pilgrimage.

This group became the church youth group. We fixed another meeting for a few weeks later and I planned to use this to explain more about the pilgrimage. I knew that so many youth groups become little more than babysitting for teenagers. The young people play snooker and listen to records while the leaders try to get God into the conversation. These young people were bored with church so I wanted to enable them to discover a fresh experience, something which was their own, something in which they could feel involved. The pilgrimage was central to this.

How: budget

I estimated I could keep the price down to about £30 per person. I wangled some money from the church council to ensure that nobody would be unable to come for lack of finance.

How: planning

It was very important to have some good leaders. We would be walking between twenty and twenty-five miles a day, sleeping the night on the floor in church halls and, unless a church along the way took pity on us and provided a meal, preparing all our own food. I therefore needed experienced help with safety, first aid, catering and, most important of all, since we planned to follow the old pilgrim routes across country as far as possible, someone who could read a map and compass.

We would also need back-up. Since the walking would be tough, to have to carry back-packs as well would be murderous. We planned for a mini-bus to carry luggage and equipment from one over-night destination to the next and then to act as support vehicle meeting the walkers at pre-arranged points throughout the day. This would mean that, if there were any emergency, we would never be too far away from assistance. In the event this proved vital. On the second day a girl in the party tripped and broke her arm. Even though we were halfway up the south Downs we were able to get her to a hospital within an hour.

I had already found one leader. The local Community Police Liaison Officer was on the church council and was a keen walker. He was also a qualified first-aider. He had a friend who was an accomplished long distance walker who, although not a Christian, agreed to come and take charge of navigation and help with the back-up. A student training for ordained ministry came to help lead the walking and my wife drove the mini-bus and helped with the back-up. I walked and we agreed to share all catering responsibilities.

Over a period of months we booked ourselves into various church halls along the route. This was quite easy to do, though

I have since become accomplished at asking the right questions to find out the actual state of a church hall. All we
required was a floor, a kitchen with a fridge and stove, toilets
and some sort of washing facilities. Most days this meant a
couple of basins. Some halls, however, are still a long way
from meeting even these modest requirements! At this stage it
was quite easy to adapt the route to find a convenient church
hall. I also found most clergy extremely willing to help. In
Canterbury we stayed at The King's School, sleeping on the
floor of their gymnasium.

When all the stops were planned I drove the route, making
sure that I knew where to find each hall. This was also a
chance to check out their facilities.

Insurance was taken out at a very reasonable price through
the Ecclesiastical Insurance Group's Parish Group Travel
Policy. A route was fixed. A menu was planned. A mini-bus
was booked. Forms and deposits came in.

How: the pilgrimage

Fourteen young people and five adults made the pilgrimage
from Chichester to Canterbury. We began early one morning
at Chichester Cathedral with a blessing from the bishop and
arrived in Canterbury six days later. Not everyone walked the
whole way. It was a very hot week and a very long way;
several suffered with blisters as well as exhaustion. A rest and
a ride in the mini-bus was very useful for some. It may well
have been a bit too far to go in one week, but most people
walked most of the way and we stressed that we were doing
this as a group. What was important was that we all arrived,
not who had walked the whole way.

Along the roads and the ancient pilgrimage footpaths of the
Downs it was a fantastic opportunity to get to know each
other. As the week went on I was able to have very profound
conversations with some of the young people. These conversations were not only about God, though the young people all
had many questions, but also about where they thought their
life was heading.

Each day we were up early and after a simple breakfast

prayed together in the open air before beginning the day's walk. Each evening after we had arrived, eaten and rested for a while we celebrated the eucharist. We experienced holy communion as food for the journey, giving us the nourishment to our hearts and wills that was needed to make the journey. We set off at about eight in the morning and sometimes would not reach our destination till seven in the evening. Even so, we always worshipped, and as the week progressed these times grew in meaning and in length. They became opportunities to share experiences about the walk and about life and a place to ask questions about where life was going and about the real significance of this journey. I had encouraged each pilgrim to carry an intention for the journey, something which they were concerned about or a person they cared for or anything which was on their heart. Slowly these were brought to God in prayer, and slowly the God who comes to meet us when we seek was discovered at our side.

Also as the week went on and the journey seemed hard the young people, quite spontaneously, began to wash one another's feet at the end of each day. In all my ministry I have never experienced such a living example of gospel truth. That it flowed from the lives of the newest of Christians and from those who, although they had been brought up in the church had only just discovered the meaning of faith, only goes to show how the church, if it wants to reach those who are outside its bounds, must also go on pilgrimage and learn again to travel light.

Arriving in Canterbury, remembering my earlier walking pilgrimages, I mentioned to the group how at Walsingham there is a chapel a mile from the shrine called the Slipper Chapel. This was the point where pilgrims of old would remove their shoes and socks to walk the last mile barefoot. As we moved into the precincts of old Canterbury they did the same. We arrived barefooted at the Cathedral to celebrate a eucharist of thanksgiving and dedication in the crypt. We were treading on holy ground. More wonderful still, we had become a holy people.

Evaluation

It was a wonderful experience of Christian community. Two of the young people were not from a church background at all. They had come along because their friends had told them about it. They were extremely sceptical (and vocal) about the religious significance of the pilgrimage, but were highly motivated about the idea of walking 150 miles. Through the experience of doing everything together for a week, and in the context of Christian community and prayer, both those people had come to faith by the end of the week and were later baptised and confirmed. Also, the adult leader who was not a Christian was confirmed the following year.

After the pilgrimage the youth group took off in the church in a way I have never known happen before or since. I am convinced it was the fellowship along the road which created the bond of love and trust that made this possible. Also, being rooted in prayer, the whole enterprise formed this group as a church. The meetings that followed the pilgrimage remained rooted in its experience. These young people discovered a way of being a church which suited their culture and aspirations and the needs of their situation. Like the very first Christians they had become 'followers of the way' (Acts 9:2).

10 SPLASH OUT

Betty Pedley

Why

'But we have no children!' was our church's cry. We knew there were many children living in the community. We saw them going to school, in the shops and the library, waiting for buses and kicking footballs on the recreation ground. We saw them walking past the church. How could we best invite them to come inside? As a church we wanted children, so we decided to take action.

When and where

We knew that we would have to make our initial contact with the children at some time other than on a Sunday. We decided to start in a small way with a one day event in the middle of the school holidays, a time when children are often bored and looking for something different to do.

Our parish hall is large and convenient, ideal for an activity day with children. We chose a day that was free from other bookings and settled on a time of 9.30 to 3.15.

How: recruitment

Encouraging the adult members of our church to take part was not easy. That was not so much because of lack of interest as lack of confidence. People have vivid memories of the Sunday schools which they attended and it can be hard for them to grasp ideas of working in a different way. It can be even harder for them to believe that they have the skill and patience to work in this way themselves.

We encouraged people to come to a 'no strings attached' planning meeting to learn more about the ideas behind our middle-of-the-week activity day. We promised support and encouragement to all volunteers. Eventually we had a firm commitment of ten adults.

Who

We decided to invite 5–11 year olds to the activity day, children who are in full time primary school. We would have liked an open door for all children but we decided to be firm and only take bookings from children in our age band. We recognised that pre-school children are too young for the kind of activities we were planning and that if we allowed them to come with older brothers and sisters it could lead to them being fretful and disruptive. Similarly, we felt that children over the age of 11 are too mature for the type of activities we were offering and they could undermine the programme through opting out and giggling.

Based on our ten volunteers, we could offer 50 places. We felt it was important to work on an adult child ratio of one to five for children aged 5–7 years, and a ratio of one to eight for children aged 8–11 years. We also ran a pre-school group for the children of helpers only and this was on the ratio of one to four.

Theme

We chose the theme 'Splash out!' Here in the north we receive a lot of rain so it was certainly a relevant title. The water theme allowed us to include activities based on the waters of baptism.

How: planning

We began planning in February. It seemed strange talking about the summer holiday with February snow on the ground and only the first few crocuses appearing in the gardens. However, in order to be well organised and to have the time to do all our planning in a relaxed way, we needed to allow ourselves plenty of time. We drew up a time scale for our planning.

During February we needed to undertake initial planning, book hall, confirm dates, secure leaders, choose theme, begin praying for the event, children and leaders. During April we needed to prepare publicity, allocate craft work preparation to leaders and other members of the congregation. During June we needed to meet for more detailed planning and progress reports. During July we needed to deal with publicity, send letters to schools early in the month, confirm places or send out regret letters before the end of term. In this way we were prepared for the event itself in August.

How: publicity

We secured the goodwill of the primary school headteachers, leaders of uniformed groups, the librarian, the local GP and practice nurse who all agreed to help publicise the event. Our publicity was designed to be attractive and eye-catching. It gave details of the event and it also clearly stated that the activities would include Christian teaching. We felt it important that parents should know exactly what they were opting in for before giving consent for their children to attend.

The publicity included a reply slip as we felt it necessary to get parental signatures, details of any health problems which we should know about, exact ages, etc. This was a great aid to our detailed planning and very important when taking responsibility for other people's children.

We placed boxes in school libraries for the reply slips. These were sealed cardboard grocery boxes painted brightly and with a slit cut in the top like a voting box. The boxes were carefully marked so that people knew exactly what they were for.

We also placed posters in prominent places, places where people stand in queues and have time to read notices. These included the fish and chip shop, the doctors surgery and the post office.

Once the posters were in place and all the handbills distributed through our chosen distribution channels, the reply slips began to be returned. We had a system of acknowledging these slips either by letter or telephone confirming that a place had been reserved for the child or that places were no longer available. This confirmation system gave us the opportunity for a friendly contact with the child's family.

How: programme

9.30	Registration, badge-making, sorting into groups
9.45	Welcome, singing, introduction to the theme and shout, game
10.10	Group activity 1
10.55	Juice and biscuit
11.00	Together time
11.30	Group activity 2
12.15	Dinner and play in safe area
1.15	Together time
1.40	Group activity 3
2.20	Group activity 4
3.00	Juice and biscuits
3.05	Together time, competition results and closing prayers
3.15	Home

How: splash out

On the day things went well. The children arrived and badges were made in the shapes of taps, umbrellas, boats, fish, raindrops and seagulls.

Together times linked the qualities of water with our experiences of water and with the waters of baptism. These times included singing and games, a shout of 'Splash out!' every time the children heard the word 'water', competitions and jokes, and later in the day the story of the storm on the lake.

Group activities involved art, craft and games based on the theme. These included activities related to water for cleansing, water for quenching thirst and water for giving life, as well as activities related to boats, fish, the rain and umbrellas.

Evaluation

It was a good day. It was a different kind of experience from anything the children had known before. It certainly challenged their preconceived ideas of the church and the people who work in its name. It was fun, it was stimulating and many asked 'When can we come again?'

In the initial planning some of our leaders had thought that there was much unnecessary organisation but by the end everyone was convinced that it was the good planning and organisation, coupled with a team of committed leaders, that made such a major contribution to a splendid day.

Follow up

After our day we felt that we had a commitment to these children and to their families. Also, having put so much time, prayer and effort into making this initial contact, we did not want to lose it again. We therefore planned our next twelve months in the church, targeting the occasions when we would contact these children and their families again.

We decided on the following activities and sent out invitations.

Harvest	Saturday morning of activities to prepare for Harvest Festival and Harvest Festival service on Sunday
October	video afternoon in the half term holidays
November	bonfire party
December	Christingle service, Crib service, and other Christmas services

February   pancake party
March   Mothering Sunday service
Easter   Good Friday service and workshop for children
Pentecost   kite making and flying, and Pentecost celebration
August   the next holiday club activity time

Personalised invitations were sent out for these activities. Some were invitations to the child alone; others were invitations to the child's family. For the video afternoon we included an invitation to bring a friend, along with a reply slip for the parents of the friend. We needed this for safety reasons and to add to our register.

We realised that the children's work leaders had to work very closely with those in the church who are responsible for outreach into the community. When families came to our events it was important that they meet as many people as possible and so have the opportunity to see the church family functioning together. We wanted our new friends to experience a quality of friendliness and acceptance from all members of the family, adults and children alike. We believe that there is a quality of experience within a truly functioning Christian family that is infectious. Some would call it holiness, some the power of the Holy Spirit and others would not try to give it a name but would know that there is something different and want to find out more.

We did not set out to provide a social calendar which would operate in competition with other organisations and agencies. We set out to provide opportunities for friendships to develop in a natural way. It was as friendships developed between the regular folk and those who had been especially invited that questions were asked and links into other church based activities became possible.

Twelve months later

By the end of the year we had offered much prayer for these children and for their families. Some had responded to every one of our invitations and we were building strong links. Some are well on their way to becoming full members of the church. Some have responded on one or two occasions and we have links with the children but not with the parents. Some families did not respond at all and we did not see the child again after the initial day.

At the end of the twelve months we revised our register. Some children had become so much a part of things that they no longer needed invitations and reminders. For those who had shown no interest, we felt that continuing with regular invitations could feel like harassment and so their names were also removed from the register. Those who had shown occasional interest were maintained on the register for invitations to be sent in the following year.

By the following February it was time to start the process once again, drawing in new children and hopefully through them linking into their families. It was hoped that the second year's activities would include as activity leaders and encouragers those who we had met through our first activity day.

Conclusions

After a year of strategic approach to outreach, we could begin to draw some important conclusions.

First, we recognised the central role of good, consistent and strategic planning. The whole strategy has been properly undergirded by consistent organisation and by prayer.

Second, we recognised that our commitment to the children whom we contacted and to their parents had to be long term. We realised that there was no direct link between activity day attendance and immediate regular Sunday attendance.

Third, we realised that, in our main priority, we were trying to communicate gospel values through natural opportunities for making friends and breaking down barriers. In this sense, specific teaching and the sharing in worship came next.

Fourth, we hope that we never lost sight of the fact that children are very special and important in their own right. We realised that we could maintain strong links with unattached children mid-week and through activity events and we welcomed that. However, we did think it was also important to see the children as part of the families to which they belong. The chances of their being able to grow in the worshipping life of the church are very slim when the rest of their family make no time for worship on Sunday. Consequently we developed our strategy which attached importance both to the child and to his or her family.

Twelve months on we certainly can no longer say 'We have no children'.

11 SAINT MARY

Angela Warwick

Why

Some members of the Parochial Church Council of Datchet, a congregation in a Berkshire commuter village, read *Children in the Way* and felt encouraged to take action. Datchet comprises a variety of people; some are traditionalists and prefer few changes, while others are adventurous and continually look for the next step forward. It is not always easy to keep both groups of people happy so, in order that the congregation was not too divided, it was important that steps be taken slowly. We decided to set up a Children in the Way follow-up group with the task of putting some of the theory from the General Synod report into action in the parish. Was it possible for this group of ordinary people to plan and deliver a day that would involve and excite people of all ages, yet not cause too many eyebrows to be raised in protest?

When

In keeping with the brief of being conservative rather than ambitious, it was agreed that the event should be part of a day, rather than a complete day. The day chosen was the Sunday of our patronal festival, a time when people had come to expect something special and slightly different in the way of a celebration. The event was to follow on after the usual morning eucharist, and was to be set up during the normal coffee time.

Where

The church building has a clear space at the back where activity tables could be set up. A small hall adjoining the church is generally used for morning coffee, and could easily be set up for sherry and lunch in between the activity time and the special service.

How: planning

The Children in the Way follow up group became the basis of the planning group for an all age event. This group of six people met several times. As the church is dedicated to St Mary the Virgin, it was decided to take as a theme events in the life of Mary as depicted in the Gospels. The main activity was to be a number of collages depicting these stories of Mary. As the planning group had little idea how much help would be forthcoming, it was important that the programme for the day be simple yet attractive.

An important task was to find and prepare leaders for the collage groups. This was not easy. The most effective method was to approach individuals, tell them about the event and ask them to offer their particular skills. The leaders were given some idea of what would be expected of them and how much time would be needed. Every effort was made to make sure the tasks did not seem too daunting or too time consuming.

How: publicity

The best publicity for the all age event was by word of mouth and personal invitation from the planning group members. Previous experience told us that people in this parish respond best to an invitation when asked individually.

Other publicity was placed in the monthly parish letter and in the weekly service and notice sheet. Organisations (adult and children) were invited to keep the day free. An air of anticipation prevailed and there was much talk about it in the weeks leading up to the big day.

How: programme

9.30   Parish eucharist
10.30   Coffee in the hall. The planning group and helpers prepared tables and equipment in the back of the church. Leaders of the collage groups were allocated tables.
10.45   Welcome, explanation of events, and collage groups
11.45   Music
12.00   Sherry and drinks (and finishing off)
12.30   Picnic lunch
2.00   Service
2.30   Finish

How: activities

Collage groups

Nine collage groups were planned, one for each of the stories in the life of Mary. A different background colour was planned for each picture.

Story	Bible reference	Colour of paper
Annunciation	Luke 1:26–38	white
Visitation	Luke 1:39–45	green
Nativity	Luke 2:1–7 (or 1–20)	red
Presentation in the Temple	Luke 2:22-38	mauve
Flight into Egypt	Matthew 2:13–15	dark green
Temple at age of 12	Luke 2:41–50	orange
Family life	Luke 2:51–52	blue
Wedding at Cana	John 2:1–10	yellow
Mary at foot of cross	John 19:25–27	black

Glue and scissors were provided, along with a wide range of collage materials: fabric, tissue paper, ribbons and lace, felt, coloured sticky paper, paints, felt tipped pens. Each group was given its own roll of kitchen paper and a black bin sack for rubbish, along with a bucket of water and a cloth. For safety reasons, materials were out of the reach of very small children.

Each group leader was allocated a story, a coloured background sheet of paper or card and some bibles. The leaders chose their own materials but the planning group encouraged them to use as wide a variety of materials as possible, in order that all the collages looked different. This involved discussion and negotiation.

Before the session, the group leaders went to their allocated tables with their background sheets and their chosen materials. The people attending wandered round informally looking at what was available, thinking about the theme and choosing which group to join. This worked well, giving a gentle start with introductions and conversation before settling down to work. Once the groups had formed, the leaders read the story with their members and worked out how they would interpret the story in collage with the given materials.

An additional small group used this time to work on an impromptu drama on the life of Mary, with one adult as the narrator reading from a simple script written in advance by two people. Members of the group mimed to the reading. It began with the twelve-year-old Jesus lost in the Temple. A popular scene was the wedding at Cana, with the bride and groom played by a courting couple and the father of the bride played by the young woman's father. The drama ended on a serious and reflective note at the foot of the cross, where Jesus told John to look after Mary. The majority of the spoken part came from the narrator standing in the pulpit, though some actors chose impromptu spoken parts. There was a big mix of ages in this group and all seemed to get on well. The drama was very thought-provoking

Music

After the collage groups, the choirmaster spent fifteen minutes teaching everyone a hymn about Mary. On this occasion the selected hymn was from Lourdes, sung to the traditional tune of 'Ave Maria'. The Walsingham Hymn or any other hymn about Mary could be used. As our chosen hymn is rather long, it was decided to sing it in sections in the service.

Lunch

At 12.00 sherry and soft drinks were served in the hall, followed by a sandwich lunch together at 12.30. There was much chat about the morning, especially about the work on the collages. The more energetic of all ages joined in some team games. These were played with balloons: balloons between the knees, balloons passed over heads, balloon type volley ball. Other people sat and watched, cheered on the teams or kept the score.

By around 1.30, people drifted back to the church to finish their collages, to look at each other's work and to display their efforts on the walls. There was of course clearing up to do.

Service

At 2.00 everyone gathered in the front of the church in a very informal act of worship. This was led by the rector whose main task was to make sure that things happened in the right order, with appropriate links between the various presentations. Although this was a vital task, he did not actually have much to say.

The service took the following form.

Hymn
Reading, Annunciation
Reading, Visitation (shortened)
Reading, Nativity
Hymn (first few verses)
Reading, Presentation in the Temple (shortened)
Reading, flight into Egypt
Drama, Jesus in the Temple aged twelve
Reading, family life
Hymn (middle verses)
Drama, wedding at Cana
Drama, words of Jesus from the cross
Short silence
Informal prayers of thanksgiving
Hymn (remaining verses)
Blessing

Each time a bible passage was read or a drama performed, the appropriate collage was viewed. Some groups felt that further explanation of the picture was necessary, and for all the collages it was important that time be given for everyone to look at what had been made. Children like to be close up to pictures so they wandered about for a closer look.

Evaluation

It worked. It was simple to organise, without being a burden for the few. About 40 people came, of all ages, some younger than 5 years and a few over 80. The families where only one partner attends church found Sunday lunch time difficult and felt they could not divide the family Sunday further by staying after church so they did not join the fun. For others, Sunday was an ideal day, especially as the event finished in time to have tea with Granny or to cut the grass.

Although the choice of collage groups was organised in a very impromptu way, people seemed happy with being able to take their time to select. It would not have been so easy with larger numbers. The selection of collage materials by the groups was also unplanned, but each group managed to produce a collage made in different materials. One was made of fabric, one of sticky paper, one of tissue paper, and some ambitious groups used a mixture of paint, paper and fabric. Many groups were quite creative with the trimmings, with lace, string, buttons and glitter.

The day was a memorable experience. As a first effort it was fun, interesting, not too long, achievable and left people wanting more.

Resources

Bible

Matthew 2:13–15 (Flight into Egypt)
Luke 1:26–38 (Annunciation)
Luke 1:39–45 (Visitation)

Luke 2:1-20 (Nativity)
Luke 2:22-38 (Presentation in the Temple)
Luke 2:41-50 (Temple at age of 12)
Luke 2:51-52 (Family life)
John 2:1-10 (Wedding at Cana)
John 19:25-27 (Mary at foot of cross)

Books

Children in the Way, London, Church House Publishing, 1988

12 NEW BEGINNINGS

Anne Faulkner

Why

Our children's event began almost by accident. It grew out of discussion at a crèche.

It is seldom easy in church life to get people to work together, admitting weaknesses and building on each other's strengths. This is true in the life of a single congregation but we, in our team of four churches in a large modern town, find it even more difficult to get people to do things together. The four district churches are socially and culturally very diverse. The parish includes established owner occupied houses, a large London over-spill council estate, an area that is predominantly Muslim, and a church congregation that is almost entirely black. We know from experience that it is easy for us to be competitive with and suspicious of each other.

One April our Parish Annual General Meeting was held on a Sunday afternoon, with tea, in an attempt to get people from the four churches to attend. In order to help parents attend the meeting, we provided a crèche for children. Because a few adults felt that the leadership of the crèche had been dumped on them at the last moment, some interesting discussions arose while we were looking after the children. We were concerned that children's events should be planned carefully, not just be allowed to happen. We came up with the idea that if we could plan together and share a children's event, we could learn from each other, we would get to know each other better, and those who led children's work might not feel so isolated and unsupported, as some clearly did at present.

We decided to try out such an event, and chose for it an afternoon in September.

Who

Our plan was for an event for children of all ages, led by adults. However, we ended up with what we can only describe as an event for people of all ages

Where

After thinking about all four church buildings, we selected the one we considered most suitable. The chairs in this church are movable, it has a good car park, there is a nearby hall, and much of the equipment that would be needed, such as painting aprons, large plastic sheets for the floor and cutting out boards, was already in place.

We planned for our event to take place in the church and hall. The registration, welcome and the opening activities would be in the church while the activity sessions could be divided between the church, the hall and outside on the grass. The vicarage kitchen was on stand-by in case of poor weather, but was not needed.

When

We first thought of the idea in April. It was discussed and approved at the June Parish Church Council. It was then put on the agendas of the District Church Councils. An open meeting for all those interested was held in July and the planning group took responsibility from then on. The actual event occurred on the first Sunday in September.

How: planning

After the idea had been approved by the Parish Church Council, letters were written to all the clergy in the team and to the District Church Councils secretaries commending the idea to them and asking for their support and encouragement. Each church was asked to advertise an open meeting to which all interested people were invited. About nine people came to this meeting and another one or two sent apologies and expressed interest. Even at this early stage the age group opened up. We had expected that the meeting would just be attended by adults, but some teenagers turned up too.

This group of interested people became the planning group and met on three further occasions. The membership varied a little but at all times there was representation from the four congregations and the teenagers remained active, enthusiastic and faithful.

The planning group decided that the event would be for an afternoon and that we would work within the constraints of The Children Act 1989 (see Appendix). That meant that the timetable would include two hours for all children, followed by worship and tea at which parents of children under eight would join us so that their children could stay. The session after tea was planned for the eight year olds and over, but would be different and informal so that younger children did not feel left out.

The chosen date in September was at the start of the new school year, so we decided that our theme would be New Beginnings. This gave us scope to think about new beginnings in plant life, new beginnings with babies, new beginnings in baptism and confirmation, new beginnings at school and in the life of organisations like Brownies and Cubs.

Members of the planning group undertook various areas of responsibility such as poster making, tea coordination, welcome leader, treasurer, first aid, games, activities and equipment. Activity leaders were discovered in a variety of ways. Some were members of the planning group, some were press-ganged clergy and some actually volunteered. Each activity leader was responsible for making sure that they had all that they needed.

How: publicity

In addition to the letter sent to the clergy and to the District Church Councils secretaries, posters were made to go up in all four churches. Because the event was aimed at children, we decided they should all receive named invitations. The invitations were produced for all four churches by one of the planning group. They included several pictures which the children were invited to colour and to bring with them when they came to the event. Although we agreed to give small prizes to everyone who returned a picture, we did not announce this. Names were written in the invitations by local people who knew the children, and these were given out from the start of August onwards.

We needed adults to help and to assist with food. We invited people in face to face conversations as this is often more effective than putting up notices or writing in pew sheets or on service papers.

How: budget

We did not want to have to charge the children for coming, and so each of the four District Church Councils was asked to make a donation of £10 and the Parochial Church Council was asked for a further £10. This also meant that the leadership teams in the parish felt committed to the project. One major budget item was food. Expenses were offered to people providing this, though many chose to donate it. The planning group appointed as a treasurer one of the teenagers. He kept an account of expenditure, which was presented to the church councils at the end after all the bills had been paid.

How: programme

1.00 Planning group arrives to set up
2.00 Children arrive – registration
      Opening game
2.15 Welcome
      Theme-setting game and opening prayers
2.45 Activity merry-go-round
3.45 Parachute games
4.00 Worship
4.30 Tea

5.00   Ending
        Informal games for older children until 6.00

How: events

Setting up

The planning group had a clear list of what needed to be done in this time so that extra help could be deployed at once and no one stood round doing nothing. Chairs had previously been cleared away from the nave of the church and so the way was clear for setting out equipment, preparing activity sessions and the welcome table, and getting tea ready.

Registration

As the children arrived they were shown where to put their coats and were taken to the reception table. Sitting at this table were four people known to the children, one person from each congregation. Each of these people had a pen of a different colour (four churches, four colours – red, blue, purple and green). The children were asked to go to the person from their church and in the appropriate colour to write their names on two labels. One was a name label to decorate and wear, the other was kept at the desk for a later activity. A complete list of children present was also made as they arrived, so that we knew who was present in case of emergencies and for our records.

Any coloured in invitations that were brought along were collected as people arrived and displayed on the wall of the church.

Once the children had finished writing labels they moved to a table where they decorated their name labels with tiny self-adhesive pictures. The labels were then fitted into plastic covers and pinned on the children.

The opening game

The children were asked to collect names of people they did

not know and to record these, with the help of adults if necessary, on sheets of paper headed 'My new friends'. The
different colours of their labels helped the younger children to
do this.

The welcome

Everyone sat together on the floor in the open space in the
middle of the church to be welcomed by one of the planning
group. Introductions were made, for example, 'Who is from
St ...? Give us a wave.' 'Who is in charge of ... (*first aid*)?
Give us a wave.'

At this stage we became aware that there were many more
adults and teenagers present than we had expected. They had
turned up to help.

Theme setting game

During the welcome, some adults had spread about 150
specially made dominoes all over the church floor. These
dominoes were made on small file index cards to show
pictures of new beginnings. There were pictures of new
babies, new toys, new school uniforms, new shoes, brides and
bridesmaids, engagement rings, new holiday experiences and
so on. Several copies of each picture had been cut from iden-
tical catalogues and glued onto cards. The children were each
given one card to start with and told to look for cards with
matching pictures. Gradually, with some hiccups and much
laughter, we made a very large domino game all round the
floor of the church. This game was obviously planned to give
children an active experience of new beginnings, but older
folk joined in with much delight, and not all of them were
even pretending to help the children.

Each child then potted a tiny plant. These had been gathered and nurtured by one of the planning group for several
months. This required careful organisation of compost, plants
and children. With each plant in its pot the children sat down
on the floor and we talked about the plant. The children
quietened down very quickly for this part. We looked at the
colours, at the shape, talked about what made it grow and how

this was a new beginning for the plant. We also talked about new beginnings at school and at home. This became our prayer time as we thanked God for new life and new beginnings by singing quietly 'Thank you God for ... new beginnings, new plants, new schools' etc.

The second labels that had been written at registration were stuck on the plant pots so that the children could take them home. These pots were then put safely on a table. At this stage we realised once more that adults and teenagers were not just helping the children but were joining in. Many of them potted their own plant to keep and take home.

Activity merry-go-round

Our coordinator of activities explained that there was a choice of things to do. Children could choose an activity and stay with it for 15 minutes, then they could move if they wished or they could remain to finish something if they preferred.

Children moved quickly to the activities and adults also selected what they wanted to do. Some adults stayed with their children, some wandered off to join in on their own. Some activity leaders found themselves with participants who were much older than they were. Two girls aged 11 and 12 agreed to lead one activity and found that it attracted adults, but they were well able to hold their own and to keep the adults in order.

One member of the planning group was responsible for keeping the merry-go-round moving every 15 minutes and for collecting strays who might wander away from a group or never reach one. In fact this was not the problem that we feared and the children were very settled and occupied.

Painting

The idea of new beginnings at baptism and confirmation was expressed in this activity. Children worked on four panels (one to go back to each church) which each showed a large cross. Hand painting was used to fill in these crosses, symbolising the hands of confirmation. Water was painted at the foot of each of the crosses and the children painted and cut out baptism candles to go round the crosses.

Collage

New beginnings were shown in four collages (again one for each church). This took the form of new babies, new plants, new houses and new gardens. Catalogues and magazines were cut up and glued in place.

Music

This session was planned so that the children could practise the music for the worship at the end. Other activities proved to be more popular so the music was not as well rehearsed as we had intended.

Clay and play dough

This was very popular both with the children and with the adults, some of whom remained with this group for the whole of the time available. We bought real clay and soft modelling material. This is expensive but it gives great pleasure and very satisfactory results. Discussion about new beginnings occurred as models were made and remade. The finished works of art were taken home at the end of the afternoon.

We offered play dough as an alternative as very small children often do not like the feel of wet, cold clay and will not use it.

Goop

We included goop just for the fun of it, and because the younger children love it. To make goop, mix a packet of corn-flour (or more if you want a lot) and about a teaspoonful of food colouring with very approximately 300 ml of water. It becomes a custard like substance that can be dripped all over a table, drawn in and then scooped up and put back in the bowl. It looks solid but feels soft to the touch. No one can believe that it leaves no mess at all. It can easily be cleared away to make a new beginning.

Although this activity, run by two young people, was intended for the very youngest children, we found that unaccompanied adults could not keep away.

Bulb planting

One of our unsuspecting clergy was persuaded to run this activity. The children planted Christmas flowering hyacinths in pots that they could take home, with the possible option of bringing the bulbs back to church when they flowered.

Bubble painting

Blowing through straws into paint and washing up liquid is great fun. Once the bubbles have been blown, paper is held over them and a picture is made. Each bubble is a new beginning which only lasts a very short while.

Parachute games

While the clearing up was done and the worship prepared, the children went outside on to the grass for some energetic games with the parachute. True to the pattern that had developed during the afternoon, many adults came straight out to join in and those who were clearing up came out as soon as they could. By the time we came to stop, all ages and all sizes were playing together, all being led by one of the older teenagers who was in charge of proceedings

Worship

One of the clergy, a member of the planning group, was asked to take responsibility for the final worship. Some of us felt that we would have liked a lay person to do this but it seemed safer and easier to use the clergy. He took trouble to include his colleagues and to involve the children and the activity leaders.

While the children had been playing with the parachute, the products of the activity sessions had been displayed all round the church. The worship started with everyone standing in a big circle in the clear space in the nave of the church. The New Beginnings Okey Cokey was sung. This had been made up to the tune of the Hokey Cokey by one of the clergy (see Appendix). In turn the activity leaders were asked to explain very briefly what had been produced by their session. As they spoke, the children took the various offerings (pictures, clay models, bulbs in pots etc.) to the altar. In between each offering we sang 'This is the way we ... make a collage/ paint a picture etc.' to the tune of 'Nuts in May'. Then we all moved into the sanctuary and joined hands round the altar to sing 'Father we adore you' very quietly. Someone said a prayer, all the clergy present gave the blessing and then everyone sang a song, as a round, to the tune of 'London's Burning'.

Tea time

All through the afternoon goodies had been arriving for tea and the member of the planning group in charge, with the group of helpers, had been busy setting up and getting ready. The children all washed their hands and sat down on the blankets on the small piece of grass between the hall and the church. When we had sung grace, tea was brought out and the children were asked to stay sitting down. This organisation worked very well. It was only the adults who walked about eating!

Ending

We ended in the hall all together. By this time it was too cool to be outside and the smallest children were quite tired. We said thank you to the people who had worked hard to get everything ready and to give us tea. We then gave a tube of sweets to every child who had returned an invitation that they had coloured.

We held hands in a circle and said good bye.

Informal games

Some children remained to play rounders and to play with the frisbee and the skipping ropes, but as most had younger brothers and sisters they nearly all went home very soon after we ended at about 5.15.

Evaluation

The planning group met for a short evaluation session at 5.45 after the clearing up was done and everyone had gone home. It was generally agreed that it had been a very good afternoon though we noted the following points for future events. The domino game was too big and took too long to finish. It would have been enough to have 100 dominoes rather than 150. Communications in the parish need to be improved. One of the four churches arranged another event for that afternoon involving the same people. Although we thought we had too much tea, it all disappeared. We did not expect or plan for so many latecomers. Perhaps this is because we started rather early for a Sunday afternoon, especially as most people had been at their own churches in the morning and had to have lunch at home before they came.

The main point of our evaluation has been addressed throughout this account. What started as an event for children led by a few adults, turned into an all age event, as teenagers and adults of all ages, men and women, arrived to make a contribution, to give support or just to enjoy it. Adults afterwards commented on how much they had enjoyed the event and what a good experience it had been for them. We wondered how many of them would have been brave enough to come if we had advertised it as an all age event? Was it because they had the children to hide behind that they felt brave enough to join in as adults?

The general feeling was, when can we have another one? How about Good Friday next year?

Resources

Songs

Father we adore you (*Mission Praise* 44)
Thank you Lord for this fine day (*Junior Praise* 232)

Books

Children's Art and Crafts, published by the Australian Women's Weekly

More Children's Art and Crafts, published by the Australian Women's Weekly

Peter Privett (ed.), *Signposts, Practical Ideas for All Age Learning*, London, National Society and Church House Publishing, 1993

Appendix

Songs

The New Beginnings Okey Cokey (to the tune of the 'Hokey Cokey'; © Peter C Faulkner)

1.   We plant some tiny seeds.
     We pull out all the weeds.
     We plant some tiny seeds
     And we water them with care.

Chorus
     We say our prayers to God,
     We turn around and wait,
     and that's what it's all about.
     Oh alleluia Father,
     Oh alleluia Jesus,
     Oh alleluia Spirit,
     Knees bend, arms out, Praise the Lord.

2.   We pile up some bricks.
     We put a roof on there.
     We pile up some bricks
     And we build them up with care.

Chorus

3.   We teach a child to talk.
     We teach a child to walk.

We teach a child to talk
And we give it loving care.

Chorus

New Beginnings (to the tune of 'London's Burning')

New beginnings, new beginnings.
Lord Jesus, Lord Jesus.
You're with us, you're with us
to the end of our days.

Prayer (for the end of the worship)

Lord we thank you for all our new beginnings.
Help us to make them grow.
Help us to know that you are always with us as we grow,
and bless those who help us.
Amen.

13 TEAM SPIRIT

Anne Faulkner

Why

The five churches in a large new town in the South of England
had difficulty in thinking of themselves as a team. Despite
their team purpose, they functioned as five separate congregations and many people regarded themselves as such. The
clergy team of eight plus a Church Army sister were
concerned about this and decided that a weekend away
together might help this difficulty. It was agreed that the
purpose of the weekend would be to give a selection of people
from all five congregations a chance to relax together, to
discover more about each other and to work out a corporate
team vision for the future.

Who

The weekend was to include a representative number of
people of all ages from all five congregations in the team.
It was also to include the clergy, some of whom would be
resident and some of whom would come and go between
leading the regular Sunday morning services in the churches.
It was clear from the start that admission could not be on a
first come first served basis but must involve more of a
balancing of ages and congregations. It was feared that
people from the larger churches would fill up the places
before the smaller, and often less confident, congregations
had a chance to offer names.

Where

It was desirable that the event should take place off-site, out of the town centre and the large housing estates where people lived. The diocesan conference centre was chosen because it was comfortable, it was in the country and it could provide a very different experience from that which people normally had at weekends. The conference centre had enough single, double and family bedrooms to accommodate the numbers of people expected, plus a bar, a lounge, group rooms and a chapel. The annexe was ideal for work with children and young people, and there was easy access to the spacious grounds outside as well as to vast areas of countryside. Because the conference centre was only about half an hour's drive away from the parish, various people would be able to attend for single sessions if needed.

When

Planning started in the late spring, after Easter, and the event took place in October. The preparations for the event were fairly intensive rather than spread over a long period of time.

How: planning

It was considered best to use an outside person as planner and leader of the weekend. All the clergy team met together with this leader to discuss their own ideas and to help her generate with an initial outline plan. The practical organisation of the weekend and the liaison between the leader, the conference centre and the people in the various district churches was all done by the staff team, but people from the parish were asked to volunteer to help in a variety of different ways.

Quite early in the planning process there was extensive discussion about how much of the event would be all age and how much would be ages working separately. The appointed leader was prepared to facilitate the all age and adult parts of the weekend, but was clear that other leaders would be necessary for any separate children's or young people's work. It was crucial that people from within the parish were found to do this as early as possible in the planning so that they could be involved in the discussions.

Three or four months before the event was due to take place, the leader presented a first draft of the programme to the staff team, discussing and developing it with them. The clergy team consulted lay people in their parishes, who came up with ideas which were then fed back to the leader. In this way the design for the event took shape and people felt that they 'owned' it rather than it being something that had been imposed upon them.

The young people rejected adult help, deciding that they wanted to lead themselves. They agreed to join in the adult sessions, but also wanted to form their own small group so that they could make a contribution to the event from their own perspective.

Once individuals had signed to attend the weekend, people were invited to become group leaders for the discussion groups. Others were asked to lead activity groups for the Saturday afternoon. These volunteers met with the leader of the weekend and the staff team, to discuss how they might work and to receive any help, support or training that was necessary.

A small committee was set up to plan the worship for the weekend. The brief for this committee was to decide what type of worship would be suitable and to invite individuals or small groups of people to take responsibility for one service.

How: publicity

Extensive publicity was given to the weekend in the parish magazine, in the pew notices, by posters in the churches and above all by word of mouth. The clergy preached about it, people talked about it, children drew pictures about it, young people planned for it. As far as possible, everyone heard that it was happening long before they were asked to actually sign up and put money into it. This generated a sense of excitement in some of the district churches, but not in all.

How: money

It was obvious that while some people would be able to afford to come to this weekend, some would not. The staff did not want the absence of money to keep people away, and they did not want families with several children to be unable to come because of the cost, and so a great deal of trouble was taken to raise money to finance those who might not be able to afford the weekend. The fund-raising events proved to be very good publicity: dances, social evenings, raffles and a whist drive all helped to provide funding.

How: programme

Friday

6.00   Arrival
7.00   Supper
8.00   Introductory session
9.00   Notices and domestic details
9.15   Evening worship

Saturday

8.00   Morning worship
8.30   Breakfast
9.30   Session 1
10.45 Coffee
11.00 Session 2
12.30 Break before lunch
1.00   Lunch
2.15   Session 3 – afternoon activities or free time
4.00   Tea
4.45   Session 4
5.45   Nursery tea for very little children
6.00   Evensong
6.45   Barn dance with buffet supper at 7.15
10.00 Evening worship

Sunday

8.00	Morning worship
8.30	Breakfast
9.30	Session 5
10.45	Coffee
11.00	Session 6
12.20	Plenary session to choose groups for worship preparation
1.00	Lunch
2.15	Group work to prepare for the closing eucharist.
3.00	Eucharist
4.00	Tea and evaluation

How: Friday

The conference centre was comfortable and warm and the welcome matched it. People arrived by car, some feeling very unsure about staying in a new place. One elderly woman arrived so anxious that she sat in the car for half an hour trying to pluck up courage to go in. She lived alone and had not spent a night away from her home for many years. In the end someone came out to accompany her through the door and to stay with her until she felt more settled. By then, she was ready to enter into the spirit of the event.

Introductory session

After supper people began to relax with the help of the bar, and by eight o'clock the whole group, people of all ages, was together in the lounge. As most people did not know each other, name labels were worn and several 'ice-breaking' games were played as an introduction. Everyone had been asked to bring a photograph of themselves as a baby and these were placed around the room for people to try to identify the owners. This was especially popular with the children.

Another activity involved people standing round the room in a large circle. They stepped into the middle of the circle if a statement applied to them. Examples of these statements included: I walk to school, I belong to St ... church, I have lived in the same house for more than 10 years. As people moved in and out of the circle they learnt quite a lot about each other in a way that was fun and non-threatening. Many people were surprised at how much they did not know about some supposedly well-known contacts within their own congregation.

This introductory session meant that all ages, even down to very small babies, started the weekend together and everybody found themselves able to participate in a way appropriate to them and at their own pace.

At 9.00 there was a short plenary session together for notices about practical details and about details of arrangements for Saturday morning, followed by a short act of evening worship in the chapel. People were then free to go to the bar, to make coffee, to go to bed, to go out for a walk or to do anything else that they wanted to do.

How: Saturday

Although the programme for Saturday morning did not officially start until the optional worship began at 8.00, the sounds of little voices and not so little voices could be heard considerably earlier than that. Some families went out to play games on the grass well before this time.

Who is in our team? (session 1)

At 9.30 the first official session began. This was for everyone of all ages. Each of the five team churches had been asked in advance to prepare a short (maximum fifteen minutes) presentation about the history and the style of their church. They could involve as few or as many people as they liked and each congregation was expected to come prepared to do this.

The presentations ranged from a straightforward delivery by one person to a visual presentation involving a number of people with drawings and pictures. Between each presentation everyone was asked to talk briefly in twos and threes about what they had learnt, what was new, and what they had recog-

nised about the life of that church. At the end of all five offerings everyone talked informally together for about ten
minutes, trying to identify differences and similarities in the
life of the churches of their parish.

Many children joined in this quite well, though some
preferred to simply play with the assortment of toys on the
carpet in the middle of the room. Some over fives even helped
with the presentations. Adults were very willing to help the
children feel part of the session and parents were not left to
cope with their children on their own. The teenagers sat
together to watch the presentations (they had declined invitations to be part of these) and talked about their perceptions of
the different district churches.

Being a team: what does that mean? (session 2)

For this session, everyone worked in age groups. The adults
were put into mixed church groups, which had been arranged
by the clergy in advance. As far as possible, each group
contained an identified leader and at least one person from
each of the five churches. Although it looked very good on
paper, there were many changes once the groups became a
reality. All groups were given a task.

The task for the adults was to talk about what they do best
as district churches and what they do best as a team. In light
of this discussion, they were asked to consider how things
could be changed and improved. Responses were recorded on
a large sheet of A1 paper.

The teenagers went away with a Polaroid camera to create
a collage display entitled 'Who's who in the team?' They were
given permission to interrupt any group to take quick
photographs of people for this display.

The children were asked to play team games, make badges
and make a poster or a banner showing all their names. What
they actually did was to draw around each other to paint an
enormously long poster of themselves as a team. The very
small children went into the crèche in an open space in the hall
where they could easily find parents who were involved in the
group work. Some children preferred to stay with their parents
in the adult groups.

Relaxing together (session 3)

The afternoon was free, given over to whatever people wanted. Some families went out by themselves while others shared cars to explore the area. There was an organised walk arranged for people who preferred that option. For those who chose to remain indoors, several activities were run: dance, drama, chorus speech, bible study, painting, clay and music. Although all of these activities were offered, not all were required. The teenagers decided to remain together and went off by themselves.

Most people returned for tea at four o'clock, but some stayed out until the next session started.

Sharing the vision (session 4)

For the first ten minutes, time was taken to share what everyone had done during the afternoon, to attempt to remember the names of those present, to re-connect with what had happened in the group work session before lunch and to generally get back into the event after the diversity of the afternoon.

All ages sat in the lounge together, with plenty of toys for the younger children on the carpet in the middle, and pens and papers, quizzes, crosswords and quiet activities for other children to do if they wished. It was accepted that children might soon lose interest in this session.

The purpose was for everyone to share together what had happened in the morning session in age groups. Each group made a brief report and added to two flip chart lists for action, one headed district churches and the other headed parish. The most dramatic part was when the children carried in their very long poster of themselves as a team. They deserved the round of applause that they received. They also offered an interesting explanation of what the poster was all about. The collage from the teenagers was not finished, but they presented what they had done so far and they managed to finish it, with some adult help, for the Sunday eucharist

This session ended in time for parents of young children to take them to the dining room for tea, so that they could go to bed when they wanted and not have to stay up for supper, although some of them had tea and supper.

The evening: social time together

The evening had been carefully planned as a social event for as many people as possible. It was a barn dance with supper in the middle. Various people, including a number of clergy, came especially for this part of the weekend. There was much exchanging of news and views, and tales told about the delights of the weekend to those who had decided that they would not come or had been unable to come. The barn dance was an in-house affair with records and one member of the congregation, who happened to be a barn dance caller, talking everyone else through the steps. The children joined in the dancing very willingly but most of the teenagers preferred to sit together in the hallway talking and supposedly doing homework.

The day ended with a short act of worship for about five minutes, held on the floor of the barn dance. Some children had gone to bed by 10.00 pm, others were taken reluctantly at the end of the barn dance and worship, but many adults lingered in the bar, drinking coffee, chatting and even going outside for a walk. History does not record at what time the teenagers finally stopped putting the world to rights and went to bed.

How: Sunday

No one was up quite so early on this morning, as all had worked hard the day before and most people had been quite late to bed. Certainly the children were not out and about quite so soon after the dawn chorus, the adults were not so keen to attend morning prayers and the teenagers were conspicuous by their absence at breakfast.

What's a Christian? (session 5)

It seemed a long time since the last session had ended at 5.45

on Saturday evening, so the day began with fun for everyone together, with a quick game about names and who we are. Then people separated into the same groups in which they had been on the Saturday morning, mixed church groups for adults, and teenagers and children in their own groups.

The adults were asked to talk about and list the qualities necessary for a Christian. That was the easy part. The hard part was that they were to present their conclusions non-verbally for everyone else to watch. Although they were allowed to introduce what they wanted to say, once they had begun the presentation they were to remain silent.

The teenage group discussed how they would present and explain Christianity to a Martian. A Martian could not be expected to have any idea about the culture or the language that is normally used to describe Christianity and the church, so this explanation required some careful thought. There was much laughter and heated discussion.

The children were asked to draw or paint a large picture of a church. It could be their own church or any church they knew. They were to label what they thought to be the important parts and then to list all the people who look after it, their positions and jobs. Then, in thinking about their own church, they were to write the names of people they knew who did those jobs. This proved to be too complicated for most of the children and instead they enjoyed drawing church buildings and designing their own futuristic worship centres. The leaders used the drawing time to talk with the children about the role of people in the work and life of the church. Younger children were asked to make a clay model of their own church, or one that they might like to worship in, or one that they had seen somewhere else.

Working on the vision (session 6)

After the coffee break everyone met together in the lounge. The children presented their pictures, drawings and models of churches and talked, a bit reluctantly, about who is needed to keep church life running.

The young people had worked very hard to produce a visual explanation that summarised Christianity as a faith of love.

Pictures cut from magazines showed suffering and celebration all over the world. In the centre of their collage they put a crowd of people stretching their hands towards the cross. The whole picture was encompassed by the supporting hands of God.

The non-verbal presentations from the adult groups were equally exciting and ingenious. One group wrote the qualities of a Christian on separate pieces of paper which were held up in turn. Another group drew a Christian and wrote the qualities round the drawing. One dramatically inclined group presented a series of mimed sketches demonstrating the qualities they had identified. Yet another group provided a series of still body sculptures showing Christian qualities. As the presentations were made, the leader for the weekend tried to write up the qualities being listed by each group so that a composite picture was formed.

This was done with some speed as adults then went back into their small groups for twenty minutes to pull all this together. The question was, taking the ideas of Saturday (sessions 2 and 3) and the qualities that are needed for the Christian life, what help is required by members of the parish to realise this vision? Each group was asked to produce two or three ideas for action that could be taken back to the Church Council to consider. These were to be written clearly on large sheets of paper.

Meanwhile the children played games outside. Some teenagers joined in the games, some went for a walk and others panicked about their homework.

Afternoon

At 12.20 everyone came to the lounge to look at the ideas for action which had been written on large sheets of paper during the previous session. They talked informally together as they looked at the suggestions: where were the similarities, which were new ideas, which ones had they tried before, how would they work? There was no further discussion as these papers were taken back to the parish for wider consultation.

There followed some discussion about preparing for the afternoon eucharist, and groups were formed to take responsibility for different parts of the service. It was agreed that people would sit in a circle for the service and that communion would be brought round rather than passed round. The difficult issue of how to include the children in the communion had been raised several times during the weekend and voices became louder at this stage. Some people felt very strongly that it was not right to leave the children out of the communion when they had been such a big part of the weekend and had given so much to the event. The discussions rumbled all through lunch.

Packing was completed, washing up after lunch finished and everyone disappeared into groups for 45 minutes to get ready for the eucharist. This was a very busy time for all, including children and teenagers.

Four activity groups from Saturday afternoon, those of dance, bible study, chorus speech and drama, spent this time finalising their particular slot in the worship. The painting and clay groups used their work to decorate the lounge ready for the service. The music group quickly rehearsed the responses for the prayers that they had learnt. Others helped to arrange the furniture and to write and duplicate the service sheet.

A decision was finally made that the children would be given communion if they wanted to receive it and if their parents agreed. It was explained to them that this was because this weekend was a special event. It would not happen when they next went to church on Sunday. This seemed a satisfactory outcome.

Everyone gathered in the lounge for the closing eucharist, including those who had come out from the parish especially for this service. (For details of the eucharist see the section on worship.)

Over tea, four large sheets of paper were spread out on flat surfaces. These were for evaluation and were labelled: what I have liked about this weekend, what I have not liked about this weekend, what I will take away with me, what I have learnt during the weekend. As people drank their tea and said their goodbyes they wrote comments on the sheets and signed them if they wished.

With many hugs and much honking of car horns, everyone drove off to start the normal week.

How: worship

All worship on the weekend was voluntary. It was organised by the worship committee and was led by those who had offered to do so in advance of the event. All volunteers were expected to resource their own service with readers and service papers if needed. The chapel owned a variety of hymn books and a set of bibles in a modern translation.

The worship times organised for this weekend were:

Friday night – Compline
Saturday morning – Morning Liturgy from the Iona Community
Saturday evening – Evensong (ASB)
Saturday night – short informal night prayers
Sunday morning – visual meditation by one of the clergy based on the writings of Julian of Norwich and the image of the hazelnut.

Sunday afternoon eucharist

Details of the order of service are given below. The teenagers' collage about the team was the centrepiece of the worship.

Call to worship by dance group
'The Lord is here: His spirit is with us'
Gloria (metric version)
Collect for the day
Old Testament reading, Exodus 14:5-31 (read by the choral speech group)
Song, How did Moses cross the Red Sea?
New Testament reading, Ephesians 4:1-8 (led by the bible study group)
Silence
Gospel, Mark 10:13-16 (read by two children)
Hymn, One more step along the world I go
Sermon, some thoughts about the weekend and the Gospel, preached by the leader of the weekend with help from the children

Prayers, informal intercessions with music led by music group

Taizé music, Ubi caritas and Adoramus te

The peace, the president gave the peace to the children who were sitting in front of the altar on the floor. The congregation was asked to wait to receive the peace from the children before greeting each other.

Offertory Hymn, Take my life and let it be

Thanksgiving Prayer, from *Patterns for Worship*

Lord's Prayer, said

Communion, taken round the circle by president and lay assistants

Silence

Hymn, Now thank we all our God

Blessing and dismissal

Evaluation

From the participants

The results of the evaluation session were written on sheets at the end of the weekend under four headings.

Some of the good things about the weekend included: acceptance of children and the provision of crèche; a wide choice of activities; the walk on Saturday afternoon; the eucharist on Sunday afternoon; midnight walks; sharing meals together; getting to know (or know better) members of the district churches.

Some of the not-so-good things about the weekend included: regret that those not present missed it all; not enough time with the groups; the need for more free time; some sessions were too long for the adults.

The things participants would take away included: energy they do not usually have at the end of a weekend; a vision of what 'team' could mean; knowledge of other people; hope of what will happen next and a vision for the future; many new friends and hope and strength.

What participants learnt included: that other people think, feel and have similar experiences; to listen to others in an attentive way; to listen to God; about other people's thoughts and feelings about faith; the necessity not to be insular as we all share a common purpose; liturgical dance is good and can enhance worship.

From the planning group

Further comments from the planning group included: not enough time for planning; too high a reliance on clergy rather than laity for planning and for organisation beforehand; more focus needed for the Saturday evening reporting back session as it ended up being too long and all too similar; teenagers would have been part of the event if they had had a leader but without being responsible to anyone it was too easy for them to opt out; never call an activity 'bible study' as the name turns people off; non verbal exercises such as drama and reporting back with pictures added a great richness to the event; the venue was excellent with the right amount of comfort and space; the aims of the event were met.

Resources

Songs

Adoramus te (Taizé)
How did Moses cross the Red Sea? (*Junior Praise* 83)
Now Thank we all our God (*Come and Praise* 38)
One more step along the world I go (*Come and Praise* 47)
Take my life and let it be (*Mission Praise* 212)
Ubi caritas (Taizé)

Bible

Exodus 14:5-31 (Crossing the Red Sea)
Mark 10:13-16 (Children are brought to Jesus)
Ephesians 4:1-8 (One body and one Spirit)

Books

Five Instant Glorias and a Creed, Rattlesden, Kevin Mayhew, 1991

Iona Community Worship Book, Glasgow, Wild Goose Publications, 1991

Patterns for Worship, London, Church House Publishing, 1995

Wee Worship Book, Glasgow, Wild Goose Publications, 1989

Julian of Norwich, *Revelations of Divine Love*, Harmondsworth,

14 SAINTS ALIVE

Margaret Dean

Why

In order to celebrate the Christian festival of All Saints, a service was planned in Guildford Cathedral on 31st October. This was to be a Christian act of worship for All Saints Eve. In keeping with this intention, we deliberately omitted all mention of Hallowe'en from the publicity and information. We wished to avoid the label 'anti-Hallowe'en' or even 'alternative-Hallowe'en' event.

Who

An invitation was given to everyone from all parishes of the diocese. As a result of this invitation, the service was attended by families, youth groups, old folk, disabled groups and uniformed organisations. Some came together as parties, some arrived alone or with just one or two others.

Where

The service was held in Guildford Cathedral and its immediate grounds.

How: planning

The complete event was planned jointly by the Diocesan Board of Education and the Diocesan Mothers' Union. The planning group met six times over a period of ten months.

There were three main areas of planning: an exhibition of artwork about the saints, the service and fireworks to follow. All three areas were planned in detail by a working group, helped by a co-ordinator whose responsibility was to assist people with the execution of their tasks. It was decided that the service would begin at 7.30 and last about 50 minutes, with fireworks from 8.30 to 8.45.

The Mothers' Union branches around the diocese were fully informed and many of them played a major part in raising funds to pay for printing and publicity and to help towards the cost of the fireworks.

How: preparation

The exhibition

In September and October, information was sent to parishes and to church schools inviting them to think in advance about the theme of All Saints and to prepare material on the saints for an exhibition around the walls of the cathedral. These items were brought to the cathedral on the actual day of the event, 31st October.

A number of possible ideas for developing the theme were suggested on an information sheet which was made available to anyone who wanted it. These suggestions included:

1. Investigate your patron saint: life, symbol, hymn, prayers, stained glass. Make a collage with the results, write a play, produce a booklet for visitors personalised for your church.
2. A saints hunt round the parish or area, including house names, streets, pubs, any other links with saints. Who were they? Why were they made saints?
3. A saints hunt around the church, inside and out, stained glass, carvings, tomb stones, books, hymns, prayers.
4. Choose a saint and collect available information. Make a display, write a play, write poetry, create a stained glass window in coloured paper.

5. What is a saint? How do you become one? Who are the saints today? Why? Who are the saints in your church? Write, draw, mime, act, sing, dance, model, arrange flowers.
6. Make a collection of saints' symbols. Why do these symbols represent them? Make badges of them, test people's knowledge of them.
7. Make a collection of hymns and prayers connected with saints. What gave the idea for the hymn or prayer?
8. Choose a modern saint and create a symbol, based on a play of his or her life.
9. Discover the patron saints of countries, trades and professions.
10. Who in your church or organisation has the name of a saint? Who were these saints originally?
11. Roger Jones' musical, 'Saints Alive' is based on Acts 1 and 2. It has 10 songs and parts for adults and children. It is published by NCEC. Plan to perform it.
12. Work out a dance sequence in which light triumphs over darkness.
13. Dress up as saints. Hold an identification parade.

Most of these items were taken, and sometimes adapted, from *Hallowe'en: an alternative* produced by the Leicester Diocese Mothers' Union. We are very grateful for their permission to use them.

The fireworks

It was decided to use a professional company, Vulcan Fireworks of Sutton, to provide the display. In 1990 they charged £1,000 for 10 minutes of performance. People attending the service were invited to donate £1 per person towards the cost of the display, and with the funds raised by the Mothers Union all expenses were covered. The company had strict regulations about fencing, marshals, car parking and insurance. We needed to arrange an alternative car park at the university, supply stewards to direct people up to the cathedral, install fencing, provide marshals and arrange public liability insurance for the crowd.

Fireworks, of course, have considerable fall out. The actual location of firing was dependent upon the wind direction on the day, to make sure the fall-out was away from the crowd. The company were prepared to fire them if it was raining, but fog would have been a problem. As it happened we had a fine night. The display was a great success, full of colour, life, unpredictability, noise, delicacy and beauty. As the cathedral is set on a hill it meant that the display could be seen, heard and enjoyed by the entire town and surrounding area.

We also had to arrange volunteers to clear up the firework remains the next morning. These remains filled two black bin bags.

How: publicity

The planning group agreed that the event should be publicised as widely as possible. Details were sent out through the clergy mailing, the children's leaders mailing, the youth leaders mailing, through the network of Mothers' Union branches, through publicity in the diocesan newspaper and through contacts with the church schools of the diocese. The event was advertised in as many places as we could think of, so that as wide a variety of people as possible heard about it.

The original poster was professionally designed but we were rather disappointed with it. We wondered if we could have produced better ourselves and would try to do so for another event. Many hundreds of posters were printed and photocopied in several sizes.

How: the event

The celebration began at 7.30 with the evening service. Guildford Cathedral is set on a hill and is therefore very conspicuous to the whole town and surrounding area. It was a fine night and the air of excitement was terrific for people climbing the hill in the dark on their way to the service and then waiting outside to get in. There was a tremendous sense of anticipation, partly because it was a new event and partly because people were glad to have a positive event to attend on that particular evening.

The theme

The service took the theme of the light of Christ coming into the world and being passed first to the apostles and then down the centuries. We featured four saints, male and female, active and contemplative. Those selected were St Mary Magdalene, St Paul, St Benedict and St Teresa of Avila, arriving in our generation. The light of Christ has been handed to us from past generations and we are now responsible for passing it on to our own generation and the children around us.

Candles and fireworks were used on the evening to portray this theme. After the first reading, a single candle was lit at the top centre of the chancel steps. This was later used to light a further four large candles on the chancel steps. Each of these four candles was lit after someone told the story of the saints and of how they had received the light of Christ and passed it on to others. Finally, everyone in the congregation received a lighted candle and left the cathedral in the darkness to be bright lights in a dark world. The firework display continued this idea.

Service

The service took the following form.

Welcome and introduction
Hymn, Praise the lord, ye heavens adore him
Greeting and opening responses
Reading, John 1:1-9
Responses
Liturgy of light
Reading, John 3:16-21
Song, A new commandment I give unto you
Presentation 1, Witnesses of the Light (St Mary Magdalene and St Paul)
Song, Spirit of God as strong as the wind

Presentation 2, Carriers of the Light (St Benedict and St
  Teresa of Avila)
Song, Colours of day
Prayers for today's saints
Offertory hymn, Church of God elect and glorious
Talk
Hymn, For all the saints
Light taken to the congregation by Scouts and Guides
Closing prayers and blessing
Song, Shine Jesus shine

The music for the service was deliberately chosen to
provide a mixture of styles and traditions for both young and
old. Some hymns were played on the organ while others were
led by a group of musicians from a local church, playing
guitars and keyboard.

For the bible readings the cathedral lights were turned very
low. After the first reading the central candle was lit.

The local Sixth Form College provided readers from their
drama courses to read the written stories of the saints. Each
story was read as though it was the saint telling how Christ had
influenced his or her own life. At the end of each reading a
candle was lit.

The prayers for today's saints were written and read by a
mother, a grandfather, a teenager and a child. Each prayer
focused on the needs of that particular age group and their
responsibilities to others. The other prayers and responses
were taken from *Iona Community Worship Book* and *Patterns
for Worship*.

The talk by the Archdeacon of Dorking was about six
minutes long and used visual images of the effects of light to
identify the responsibilities of Christians, today's saints, to
spread the light.

Before the closing prayers, some Scouts and Guides distributed candles to the congregation. Other Scouts and Guides lit
their own candles from those on the chancel steps and used
these to light the candles in the congregation.

Evaluation

The event was a great success and an exciting and happy evening was experienced by all those who attended.

Our chief difficulty was numbers. We had no idea how many people would arrive. We had to cope with 2,000 people packed into a cathedral that should seat only 1100; there was standing room only and 500 more people waited outside, while 250 went home.

Since then we have had another similar occasion and asked people to book seats. This was not satisfactory either as we had to turn some people away beforehand and others who had booked did not come. More recently we have encouraged deaneries and parishes to provide their own local occasions instead, and thus reach out to and include even more people. This changes the nature and purpose of the event and loses the concept of the churches of the diocese doing something together.

Resources

Songs

A new commandment I give unto you (Mission *Praise* 283)
Church of God elect and glorious (*Hymns for the People* 54)
Colours of day dawn into the mind (*Come and Praise* 80)
For all the saints (*Hymns Ancient and Modern New Standard* 305)
Praise the lord, ye heavens adore him (*Come and Praise* 35)
Shine Jesus shine (*Let's Praise* 120)
Spirit of God as strong as the wind (*Come and Praise* 63)

Bible

John 1:1–9 (The Light shines in the darkness)
John 3:16–21 (The Light has come into the world)

Books

Hallowe'en: an alternative (ideas for keeping the eve of All Saints' day as a Christian festival), Leicester, Mothers' Union Leicester Diocese, 1986 (revised 1996)

Iona Community Worship Book, Glasgow, Wild Goose Publications, 1991

Patterns for Worship, London, Church House Publishing, 1995

Michael Perry (ed.), *The Dramatised Bible*, London, Marshall Pickering and Bible Society

15 FIRE! FIRE!

Gill Ambrose

Why

In a year when 5th November happened to fall on a Saturday, we held a one day club ending with a parish supper, bonfire and fireworks. The theme, *Fire! Fire!* was chosen to relate to contemporary interest and explore the biblical imagery of fire and flames. Any Saturday close to 5th November would be workable and with some adaptation the theme could also conveniently work as a way of celebrating Pentecost.

Images of fire and flames pervade the scriptures. Some are concrete like St Paul and the snake on the island of Malta (Acts 28:1–6); some are mystical, for example, Moses and the Burning Bush (Exodus 3:1–6). In St John's resurrection story of Jesus on the shore of Lake Tiberias (John 21:1–14) both elements are present.

It is helpful for young people to encounter these stories in a thematic context and, of course, it can be great fun too. It also helps to develop awareness that there are major themes and images which are present throughout the biblical story and, indeed, beyond it. The opportunity to begin to confront and make meaning from a powerful image such as fire is important in the development of a capacity to think and reflect theologically. The value of a whole day project is that individuals are able to encounter a variety of experiences and work in a number of different media.

Fire is a powerful thing, both materially and symbolically. In these days of central heating and electric light, the fascination of the naked flames of bonfire or candle should not be underestimated. The candle flame still draws us to worship and the campfire still draws us together. The candle-lit church and the Easter fire continue to evoke wonder. It is appropriate, then, to explore the image of God's spirit in the flames of the burning bush (Exodus 3:1-6) or the tongues of fire at Pentecost (Acts 2:1-4); or to learn of Elijah challenging the prophets of Baal (I Kings 18:20-18) and Paul warming himself beside a fire after being shipwrecked (Acts 28:1-10).

Where

In addition to the church which is modern and has no pews, we were lucky to be able to use the modern community centre next door. There was a green outside and a nearby garden was used for the bonfire. The community centre gave us a hall with a stage, two other rooms and a kitchen. The nave of the church was divided up into group spaces by chairs. The church and community centre complex were right in the centre of an estate of private housing for probably 5,000 people or so, on the edge of a northern city, with buildings dating from the 1930s to the present day.

Timing

The day began at 10.30 and children brought a sandwich lunch which they ate at 12.45. The parish supper was at 5.00 and the bonfire was lit at 6.00. Fireworks (each church family brought a few which were then all contributed to a central pool and lit by two people behind a specially constructed low barrier) lasted from 7.00 until 8.00 allowing younger families to go home to bed. Several older families and a group of teenagers were still sitting on logs round the fire at 9.15 deep in conversation.

How: publicity

An A5 brochure was prepared. The front was an eye catching flier and further details were given on the inside page. The back page was a registration form. This required the following information to be completed: name, age and address of the child, together with the name of the family doctor and a request for information about any particular medical condition which might present difficulty during the day. This was followed by a statement of parental consent for the child to take part in the day's activities and for the leaders to act *in loco parentis* where necessary. Here is an example:

> I give permission for my child.................. to attend the *Fire, Fire!* day and to take part in all the activities which constitute part of the day, including time spent off the church premises in the care of an adult, and I authorise................*(name of leader)* to give permission to the doctor in charge to undertake whatever treatment is considered necessary for my son/daughter should the need arise.

The form required a parent's signature and details of where they could be contacted on the day if they were not at home. The rest of the form supplied a list of afternoon activity options for which the children were asked to give first and second preferences.

The brochures were distributed through all children's groups which used the community centre and through the primary school. They were also available in the local post office.

How: planning

Planning started with a small group of four people. One was a children's worker in the church, two were parents from the congregation and one was a local teacher willing to take part in a one-off event. This core planning group met for the first time three months in advance, brainstormed the theme and drew up an outline plan for the day. A list of tasks to be completed in the next month was drawn up and allocated between the members:

> booking buildings and spaces to be used;
> liaising with the church congregation and recruiting workers;

planning the next meeting to which leaders and helpers would be invited and asked to make a specific commitment;
planning, publicity and brochure design;
planning and organising resources and equipment;
further planning on content and design of the day.

The second planning meeting took place in the community centre two months before the event. All adults and young people who had offered their help were invited. Those who attended were given a sheet which explained the aim of the day and an outline timetable. Further ideas were gathered from those present at the meeting and then worked into the overall plan. Workers were invited to sign up with a definite commitment as group leaders or helpers, caterers or to give physical help with preparation and clearing up.

Outline plans were given to group leaders and helpers who then agreed to meet to make detailed plans. Rooms and spaces were allocated for morning and afternoon groups and the maximum number of participants fixed, dependent upon the number of leaders and helpers available. This was done approximately at this meeting and then refined later by the core planning group when contact had been made with a few people unable to be present at this second planning meeting.

This was a long meeting. A great deal of planning was packed into one evening, still leaving loose ends to be tied up by the core planning group. It might have been better done in two sessions but, as it is very difficult to get people together at all, it was agreed on this occasion to opt for one long meeting.

From six weeks beforehand group leaders and helpers met together to complete their plans and gather materials.

The local authority social services under eights adviser was informed of the event. An insurance check was made. It is always sensible to check, in detail, with the insurance company that the church insurance policy covers the day's activities.

One month before the event brochures were taken to the distribution points. Registration details were to be returned at least a week before the event.

The congregation was asked for their prayers and to

contribute towards the materials needed. A list of suggested items looked something like this:

> paper, paint, card, large pieces of plain fabric, baking utensils and things to burn on our bonfire.

Once we had enrolled as many children as we could cope with, a note was sent to unsuccessful applicants.

A meeting of group leaders was held a week before the event, at which morning and afternoon groups were fixed and lists of participants created. There was final liaison with the caterers. Last minute problems were ironed out and final purchases arranged.

How: programme

10.30	Registration and icebreaker
10.45	Singing
11.00	Exploring the bible
12.00	Singing
12.15	Games
12.45	Lunch
1.30	Activity 1
2.30	Activity 2
3.30	Activity 3
4.30	Video
5.00	Singing and litany
6.00	Supper

How: morning

Registration and icebreaker

Upon arrival and registration, everyone was given a large conference badge with his or her name on. These were to be decorated with flames. An icebreaker game followed. This was *Autographs* which keeps people (older children can help tinies) occupied while others are arriving. Here's how to play it.

Each participant is given a sheet on which there are nine labelled boxes. They are to find a person qualified to sign each box. Adults should be available to sign as well as children. On this occasion boxes might be, for example:

someone with an open fire at home;
someone who has seen a steam engine;
someone who has a gas cooker at home;
someone who is wearing red;
someone who has the initial F;
someone who has touched a fire engine.

Singing

Everyone came together in the hall. We sang 'London's burning' together first and then split into an increasing number of smaller and smaller groups to sing as a round, just for fun. We then sang 'Light up the fire', which became the theme song for the day.

Exploring the bible

We separated into the pre-arranged age based groups to explore some bible stories in which fire features (see Resources). The follow up to each story consisted of a discussion and reflection on the story, trying to understand the feelings and reactions of the characters involved. This was followed by drama/role play. Some groups worked together as a whole, others divided into smaller groups or pairs depending on the nature of their story. For the last 15 minutes of the hour long session the groups were paired to present their dramas to each other.

Singing

At 12.00 there was a plenary session in the hall. The children sang 'Light up the fire' again and learnt a new song which fitted the fire theme. The singing was followed by a five minute sketch which had been produced by a group of teenagers as pure entertainment. It was not on the fire theme but it did have a Christian message.

Games

At 12.15 the children had a choice between parachute games in the hall or football on the green. It is important to allow energy to be used up. It is usually possible to borrow a parachute for games either from a local authority youth club or a church resource centre.

Lunch

For lunch the children ate their own sandwiches. We supplied squash. We also supplied things to do for fast eaters: puzzles and pictures to colour and more football (under supervision) for the very energetic.

How: afternoon activities

The afternoon had three successive fifty minute activity sessions with ten minute change-over periods between them. Children had advised their afternoon preferences on their registration forms and the groups were created beforehand and displayed on huge sheets of paper, so everyone knew where they were going. However, some verbal organisation of the children was also necessary.

Bonfire building

This was very popular and most people had a turn in one of the three sessions. Men (some of whom were normally reluctant to work with children) were happy to supervise this. It also involved collecting items to burn from some houses in the parish; this was done under very careful supervision.

Cooking

Gingerbread, biscuits and toffee were prepared for the evening bonfire party by the older children under very careful supervision. The younger children made cornflake cakes, also eaten in the evening. (There were two sessions only to free the kitchen for supper preparation during the last hour.)

Dance

A couple of people who are keen on creative dance ran this session. The theme lends itself to all sorts of imaginative possibilities. One good example was the interpretation of being in the presence of fire – the warmth given in the cold by a bonfire, the comfort and intimacy bestowed on a group around the hearth, the peace instilled by a candle flame, the fascination of a great star. Then there is the opportunity to enact fire through movement – the flickering of flames, the engulfing and destruction of objects by fire. This might move to the interpretation of a story (or part of a story) or poem, for example, Peter's denial beside the fire in the courtyard of the high priest's house (Luke 22:54–62), Elijah's challenge to the priests of Baal (I Kings 18:20–40) or the story of St Patrick's Easter defiance of Laoghaire (which is described in most biographies of Patrick).

Lego

With a huge box of mixed Lego each group chose to create something relevant to the theme: Paul's ship (Acts 28:1–10), the burning fiery furnace and Nebuchadnezzar's palace (Daniel 3).

Art

Three enormous painting/collages were planned and produced, one by each group, with the titles: 'Fire gives energy', 'Fire makes', 'Fire beauty'. Some children also produced posters warning of the dangers of fire.

Banners

These were made with felt on sheeting, cut ready to size. The children designed templates on card; these were transferred to felt and laid out on the sheeting until an effective design was achieved. The felt was then stuck onto the sheeting using a suitable adhesive. All the banners were based on the biblical fire stories used in the morning.

Puzzles

This was a group for children who enjoy puzzles. They were supplied with word searches, dot to dots and bible quiz questions loosely linked with the fire theme.

Modelling

The media used for modelling were Fimo and modelling clay. Ready made examples were supplied and children chose something to make on this basis. As the materials are expensive they were encouraged to perfect one item. A group of small children also worked with playdough.

Badge-making and bookmarks

A badge-making kit was hired and a set of prepared bookmarks with quotations which could be coloured and illustrated was supplied. These were given out by the children to the congregation at Sunday morning's eucharist. Many of the quotations were taken from hymns: identifying possibilities would be a good task for a housebound person who could thereby contribute to the day. The lettering was done with a computer desk top publishing programme, although a less sophisticated programme could have been used.

How: evening

Plenary session

Between 4.30 and 5.30 there was a plenary session in the hall. Everyone gathered together to watch a video for half an hour while the church and the rest of the community centre were cleared up. Parents and other adults arrived and sat at the back during this time. At 5.00 they then joined in singing the songs the children had learnt. The session was drawn to a close with a simple fire litany led by the parish priest.

Display

Most of the work done by the children was carried to the church and arranged for display at the following day's service. Although this task was not quite completed in this period, it did not take long to complete once the bonfire was over. Models were displayed on window sills, the three paintings were attached to canes and then hung, using string, on the walls. The banners stood at the back of the church and were carried in procession at the next morning's service. The completed puzzles were laid out on tables at the back of the church also. This was done by some of the day's leaders and helpers, together with some of the children and a team of adults who had specifically volunteered for this task.

Supper

Supper was served in the hall. It was a simple meal of traditional 'bonfire food', soup, jacket potatoes and sausages, followed by a drink. We used disposable cups and plates and people ate jacket potatoes and hot dogs with their fingers to minimise washing up. We burnt the resulting rubbish on the bonfire. Over this time the children were also able to take their parents around the two buildings (the church and the community centre) to see the work which had been done.

As they left the hall for the bonfire, each family received an invitation to the following morning's parish eucharist.

How: parish eucharist

A special service had been planned earlier using the fire theme. One drama group and one afternoon dance group illustrated the bible readings. This is always a risky business of course, as one is never quite sure who will turn up for the 'performance'. We guarded against disaster, however, by careful planning. In the drama group, mime was used to a text read out by one person.

During the Saturday session the main parts were played by several children in turn so that everyone knew what was expected of each part. Movement was kept very simple. On Sunday morning the children were asked to come early to practise, and final allocation of roles was only then decided. The dance group performed the story of Elijah's challenge to the priests of Baal which had only one 'solo' role so it really did not matter how many people actually turned up. Children from among our regular congregation had been chosen to read lessons and prayers: it was important that this was done confidently and well, rather than choosing children on the Saturday to whom the Sunday situation might be strange.

Resources

Songs

Colours of day dawn into the mind (*Come and Praise* 55)
It only takes a spark to get the fire going (*Mission Praise* 111)
Shine Jesus shine (*Let's Praise* 120)
Thank you Lord for this new day (*Junior Praise* 232) (make up new verses about fire, heat, light and so on)

Bible

Genesis 22:1–18 (Abraham and Isaac)
Exodus 3:1–6 (Moses and the burning bush)
Daniel 3:1–30 (The burning fiery furnace)
1 Kings 18:20–40 (Elijah and the prophets of Baal)
2 Kings 2:1–18 (Elijah leaves the world)
Luke 22:54–62 (Peter's denial)
John 21:1–14 (Jesus appears on the lake shore)
Acts 2:1–13 or 21 (Pentecost)
Acts 28:1–10 (Paul on the island of Malta)

Books

It is important that the bible stories are well told. Each group leader chose his or her own presentation; some told the story in their own words, others used bible story books. With older children it is often possible to use the story directly from the bible but it is often necessary to set the story in context and many of the retellings do this well. The following are excellent and recommended:

Palm Tree Press Bible Stories series, Rattlesden, Palm Tree Press

A Dale, *Winding Quest*, Oxford, Oxford University Press, 1972

A Dale, *New World*, Oxford, Oxford University Press, 1967

S Hastings, *The Children's Illustrated Bible*, London, Dorling Kindersley Publishers, 1994

G Marshall-Taylor, *Illustrated Children's Bible*, London, Octopus Books, 1980

J G Priestley, *Bible Stories for Classroom and Assembly: the Old Testament*, Exeter, Religious Education Press, 1981

J G Priestley, *Bible Stories for Classroom and Assembly: the New Testament*, Exeter, Religious Education Press, 1992

Appendices

1 CHILDREN AND THE LAW

Marion Richards

Introduction

The Children Act 1989 was enacted to reform the law relating to children; to provide for local authority services for children in need and others; to amend the law with respect to children's homes, community homes, voluntary homes and voluntary organisations; to make provision with respect to fostering, child minding and day care for young children and adoption, and for connected purposes.

What does the Children Act present?

Anyone who has access to and is responsible for children, in whatever role, must comply with the requirements outlined in the above introductory statement of the Children Act 1989. The requirements of the act apply to local authority services and to privately run and voluntary organisations.

The Children Act, which took effect from October 1991, has been described as the most significant reform of legislation relating to children in our times. It has been designed to support and encourage good practice and safety in all aspects of work and involvement with children. Whilst this act is rigorous in its requirements it muse be welcomed as a guardian for the welfare of all children

The two main aims behind this act are to make the law, as it relates to children, simpler to use and, in action, more appropriate to the true needs of children. The act contains the following main principles.

- The welfare of the child must be the paramount consideration.
- Children should be brought up in their families wherever possible. Moving them must be a last resort. If moved away then the aim is to return a child as soon as possible.
- Local Authorities have a duty to provide for children in need.
- Partnership and integration with parents are key aims in this act. Services provided must be appropriate to the child's race, culture and linguistic background.
- Children should be safe and protected when necessary by intervention. Intervention by local authorities must be open to challenge.
- Substitute care, in place of parental care, should be of a high quality.
- Children must be consulted and kept informed. They are to be involved in decisions which affect them.
- Situations where children are cared for away from home must be open to scrutiny.
- The concept of a parental responsibility replaces that of parental right. A child can no longer be seen as a parent's possession. But a parent's responsibility for a child never lapses.
- Court procedures and decisions must be responsive to the needs of children. Flexibility is stressed; a principle of 'no-delay' is introduced and court orders are to be avoided unless it is better for the child that an order be made.

What do these principles mean to those working with children?

Those involved in ministry to children, whether salaried or on a voluntary basis for the church, must be aware of and uphold the principles set out in the Children Act.

The first principle underpins the ethos of the whole act in its statement on the necessity for the welfare of the child to be always paramount. The further statements focus on the major issues which arise in the nurture and care for children when their welfare is considered.

The following principles take into account all aspects of the child's welfare, the concerns and actions which can be seen to cover the whole provision for the child, including protection from any form of abuse or harm. Protecting the child from physical, emotional and sexual abuse or neglect is critical if the child's welfare is to be a happy, fulfilling experience which encourages healthy emotional, social, physical, academic and spiritual growth.

Ministry to children aims to provide experiences for children which will promote spiritual growth and the development of the whole child. In this respect, the church makes decisions on the provision of Sunday school, junior church, confirmation classes, family services, training, holiday camps and other activities. All too often this provision is planned in light of criteria based on priorities other than the child centred approach outlined in the Children Act. Priorities may include answering the needs of the existing structure of the parish system, the needs of the liturgy, the perceived needs of the children, and the needs of other groups which are given priority status in the work of the church (for example, church councils).

However, these organisational factors can be very difficult to change and the development of new attitudes often requires a great deal of support and help if the welfare of children is to be truly paramount in the decisions made for their provision.

Equally important is the identification of what is truly required to provide appropriate experiences for the children. Here, the Children Act presents the principle of giving children information and allowing them the opportunity to be involved in decisions which affect them. In ministry to children, talking to them about the churches' ministry and a sensitive 'hearing' of their requests may develop the interest and participation of young people in the Christian faith today.

If, then, the activities prepared for children in the churches care are relevant to the true needs of the children and are given high priority in any diocesan or parish plan, one must ensure that the critical issue of safety of the child is addressed and embedded in any parish policy in working with children.

Safe from harm

The Children Act clearly outlines procedures which must be carried out to ensure the safety of children. The good practice specified below is based on recommendations provided by the Home Office document *Safe from Harm: code of practice for safeguarding the welfare of children in voluntary organisations in England and Wales.*

All organisations should have a written clear policy on the protection of children in their care. Drawing on the guidelines of the Home Office document *Safe from Harm*, Parochial Church Councils should prepare a clear policy statement for ensuring the safety of children. Such a statement might include the following points.

- This church is committed to the welfare, nurturing and safekeeping of children.
- This church is therefore committed to supporting and resourcing those who work with children.
- No one will be expected to work in this church with children unsupported.
- This church will ensure that those who work with children, and those in whom children place their trust, know how to handle a situation where a child or young person is considered to be at risk through abuse or neglect.
- Children are part of this church today, have much to give as well as receive, and will be listened to. In worship, learning, teaching, evangelism, we will respect the wishes and feelings of the children.
- This church is committed to providing a safe, warm and friendly environment for all.

What is child abuse?

The abuse of children and young people can occur among families of any background and within any institutions, even those statutory bodies and structures set up to protect children.

An allegation of abuse against a child, even an anonymous phone call, will be acted on by Social Services or NSPCC.

Along with the police these agencies have powers to intervene. Other key agencies are Health and Education who will monitor and make referrals. It is important that people know the procedure and know their own limits. If there are reasonable grounds to suspect that a child is being abused in any way, this should be reported immediately to Social Services. If there is some doubt then it is possible to discuss such things in confidence without necessarily disclosing the name of the child involved. It must be stressed that it is not for the clergy or lay leaders to launch into further investigations in what may be a criminal action.

The document *Working Together: a guide to arrangements for inter-agency collaboration for the protection of children from abuse* (published by the DHSS in July 1988) outlines the following categories of registration for abuse.

- *Neglect:* the persistent or severe neglect of a child (for example by exposure to any kind of danger, including cold and starvation) which results in serious impairment of the child's health or development, including non-organic failure to thrive.
- *Physical Abuse:* physical injury to a child, including deliberate poisoning, where there is definite knowledge, or reasonable suspicion, that the injury was inflicted or knowingly not prevented.
- *Sexual Abuse:* the involvement of dependent, developmentally immature children and adolescents in sexual activities they do not truly comprehend, to which they are unable to give informed consent, or that violate the social taboos of family roles.
- *Emotional Abuse:* the severe adverse effects on the behaviour and emotional development of a child caused by persistent or severe emotional ill-treatment or rejection. All abuse involves some emotional ill-treatment; this category should be used where it is the main or sole form of abuse.
- *Grave Concern:* children whose situations do not currently fit the above categories, but where social and medical assessments indicate that they are at significant risk of abuse. This could include situations where another child in

the household has been harmed or the household contains a known abuser.

The selection of personnel

One of the major issues which arises in child protection is the state of trust to which all adults in a child's life must commit themselves. Those who have children in their care must ensure that trust is not betrayed.

Here, *Safe from Harm* states that care must be taken at all times in the recruitment of paid persons and volunteers intending to work with children. It is legally permissible to enquire about past criminal or civil offences to ensure the appointment of appropriate persons to be responsible for children. If the selection procedure identifies circumstances in which the welfare of children has been previously put at risk by a candidate, then his or her name may be referred for inclusion in the index held by the Department of Health.

In order that this process is always put into practice, proper guidelines on the implementation of appropriate procedures when appointing candidates should be available to all selection panels. All candidates for appointments should be asked to provide two references and to consent to a police check. All such declarations should be kept in a safe place agreed upon by the organisation which is responsible for the children in their charge. Most regional or national church structures now provide a recommended proforma for this purpose.

Once appointed to a specific task, it is recommended that a contract is signed by adults working with children and by the supervising minister. Such a contract might include the following points.

- Thank you for agreeing to work as part of this church's overall care for children and young people.
- We put a very high value on all work with children and young people. We want to make sure you know the resources and support available to you. We intend that you should not work unsupported or unsupervised.
- The particular responsibilities of your job have been

discussed with you in detail. Any further questions that arise from time to time can be discussed with *named individual*.

● Once a year we will meet with you to talk about your work with children and young people and, if you wish to continue, we would want you to develop your skills. Training opportunities will, therefore, be discussed with you.

● Work with children and young people is a responsibility but also brings enormous rewards. Have fun!

● *A personal note*: I welcome you to this post and assure you of the continuing prayerful support of the church.

A backup situation is recommended in that the work of any organisation is planned in such a way as to minimise situations where the abuse of children may occur. Adults should always be accompanied by another adult when working with children. This can be a parent or member of the parish who is willing to support. There are two aims here, the major aim to protect children but also to protect the adult in the situation from any false accusations which may arise.

It is important that all staff are trained in the prevention of child abuse, in order that they may be fully aware of the issues surrounding the supervision of children.

Intervention procedures

Any system of child protection must ensure that children have the facility to appeal to an independent person if concerned about another adult's behaviour. The person chosen for this role should be other than those directly concerned with the child in a teaching or learning situation. This will enable intervention on behalf of the child to take place appropriately if necessary.

If a case of child abuse is reported, then it is critical that all those directly or indirectly involved with the child must be aware of the reporting procedures. This is a difficult and sensitive area with which to deal. The welfare of the child comes first, so the procedure which reports child abuse should be put into action immediately if an incident is brought to light. It is essential that the policy for child protection clearly outlines the reporting procedures to follow. Any confusion in procedures could have a disastrous effect on all concerned.

Positive statements of abuse must be reported directly through the appropriate channels of communications, swiftly, sensitively and carefully with the needs of the child in mind. However, rumour of behaviours may need to be explored more fully before the reporting procedure is put into practice, and so clear guidelines for this aspect of the provision in Child Protection must be drawn up.

Supervision

Safe from Harm encourages the use of appropriate supervision to aid the implementation of a safe provision for children. To ensure the safety of the child the following supervision ratios have been recommended. For under 2 year olds there should be one adult for every three children; for 2–3 year olds there should be one adult for every four children; for 3–7 year olds there should be one adult for every eight children; for those over the age of 8 there should be one adult for every thirty children. Under 18s may not be included in the staff ratio and may not be put in charge of a group.

It is generally recommended that, as far as possible, a mixed group of children (boys and girls) should be supervised by both male and female adults.

Insurance

It is important to assure that adequate insurance cover is in place both for children and for adult leaders. People who are *paid* to work with children are, in the eyes of the law, regarded as employees. For this reason the specific requirements for Employer's Liability must be met. When children are passengers in private vehicles, these vehicles must be properly insured. The vehicle should not be used to carry more than the manufacturer's stated maximum number of passengers. Parental consent should be given in writing before transport is used.

Safe accommodation

Safe from Harm outlines the obligation of organisations to provide safe accommodation for children in their care. The venues for meetings must be of a high recommended standard and safe for the children. Strangers or unauthorised visitors should not be able to enter premises. Once on premises the children must not be allowed to leave unless they are supervised. If a child needs to leave, only an authorised leader should be allowed to accompany that child. At least three adults should be present at any group meeting. It is not recommended that a group should be led by one person on his or her own. Collection of children at the end of a session must be supervised with care to ensure that no unauthorised person leaves with a child.

Situations where children are cared for away from home must be open to scrutiny. The Children Act requires that all organisations caring for children under 8 years old for two hours or more must register. In a home this will only apply if offered for reward, but elsewhere it applies whether for reward or not.

Facilities which are provided for less than six days each year are exempt, but the local authority social services department must be informed in advance of the intention to provide any facilities which involve the care of under 8s for more than two hours, even though a registration is not required.

The registration will check the following factors: the person offering care; the suitability and safety of the premises; the other people who are employed on the premises where the care is offered are fit to be in the 'proximity' of children.

There are additional safety requirements which need to be observed for events which include overnight stays, even when church halls or schools are used for this purpose. For example, exits need to be properly signed and illuminated, fire drills need to be conducted, and appropriate information needs to be available for medical support.

The quality of provision for children

The Act requires that the quality of care for children must be of a high level. By listening to the children in discussion about their needs, ensuring the system places them high on the agenda, clear guidelines are followed on the appointment of personnel to work with them and the provision of safe premises provides a good start for quality provision.

Children bring with them, to any situation, a variety of backgrounds, cultures, language and religious experience. Any provision for them must take into consideration the children's individual experiences, family lifestyles and linguistic background. Only by listening and taking time to know each child can one answer their needs when in our care. Differing values and attitudes may be present which represent, for the individual child, the 'truth' of how things are. Sensitive handling of similarities and differences in individuals is an important aspect of caring for children, especially in the growth of faith. Getting to know the families is an important aspect of successful work with children.

Involvement of parents and families

The Children Act states clearly that 'partnership and integration' are key words in helping and supporting parents in the provision for children. Clearly, the young child is unable to make decisions about his or her welfare though, as the act recommends, the child will be informed and consulted about decisions which affect them. It is, ultimately, the adults in the child's life who must take the responsibility for those decisions.

The code makes it clear that a parent's 'responsibility will never lapse, even when responsibility is given to another person by a court, except in cases of adoption'. It is important to ensure all issues which arise for children are considered by both the organisation involved and the parent or guardian.

Main obligations for organisations working with children

In order to implement the Children Act as it is intended, to protect the children with whom we work and to make their needs paramount at all times, it is important that everyone makes themselves aware of the obligations the Act puts upon them.

Organisations must ensure there is a clear child protection policy for those working with children and ensure that the policy is fully implemented at all times. All decisions made on their behalf must place their welfare paramount to all else. The children must be accommodated in safe premises, cared for by responsible, trustworthy persons, be listened to and informed, and the whole provision for them must be of a high quality at all times.

The whole body of people who are responsible for children must take up the obligations laid down by the Children Act and so ensure a happy, fulfilling and safe life for the children in their care.

Advice and further information about the Children Act 1989 will be available from your Diocesan Office or from your local Social Services department.

Safe from harm check list

The following check list may help to ensure that the proper provisions are in place.

- Is First Aid available during all activities?
- Is there an up-to-date First Aid Kit available both on the premises and for activities away from the premises?
- Do leaders know who the First Aiders are and where they can be contacted?
- Are all accidents recorded?
- Do regular fire drills take place?
- Are fire notices displayed informing people what to do in case of fire?
- Are fire appliances suitable and serviced regularly?
- Has the local Fire Prevention Officer visited the premises?
- Is there suitable access and provision made for disabled people?
- Is a register kept of all those in attendance?
- Has a parental consent form and health form been completed for each child/young person?

- Are those working with children/young people suitable?
- Have youth and children's leaders been properly introduced to the work, adequately supported and offered training?
- Do youth and children's leaders in the church know what to do if a child/young person tells them of abuse?
- Are adult/child ratios appropriate for the group and for the activity?
- Are the places where children/young people meet safe and secure from unwelcome people?
- Is it possible for children/young people to 'slip' outside without leaders noticing?
- Is this check list reviewed annually?

Acknowledgement

Some material has been taken from *Better Safe Than Sorry* with the permission of the Training and Parish Resources Department of the Diocese of Oxford.

2 FAMILY SERVICES

Leslie J Francis

Context

In one sense I have always wanted the main focus of the Sunday worship of my churches to be the parish communion. The flexibility of modern eucharistic rites allows a great variety in the ways in which the parish communion can be presented. On some occasions the parish communion can be free and child-centred. An abbreviated rite can give space for young people to prepare an extended ministry of the word in song, dance and drama. Opportunities can be given for young people to create their own prayers of intercessions and thanksgivings and to prepare a nave table for the eucharistic prayer. On other occasions the parish communion can be completely formal and traditional in its presentation.

The great strength is that these two extremes are bound together with the same basic structure and the same essential components. The continuity between the child-centred presentation and the traditional presentation of the parish communion is expressed through actually using, for example, the same collect for purity and the same eucharistic prayer. Essentially the worshipping community is participating in the same characteristic liturgy of the people of God, presented in two rather different ways.

At the same time, I have also needed to recognise that the parish communion is not the appropriate form of liturgy to meet all the worship needs of the local church. There is a range of situations in which a different liturgical form is necessary and in which it is equally inappropriate to use the offices of Morning Prayer and Evening Prayer in all their various forms. It is this experienced need which stimulates

Anglican parishes to experiment with forms of 'family services'.

Discovery

After I had been in one of my rural parishes for some time, the Parochial Church Council decided to review the pattern of services so we could try to assess whether the village church was ministering to the local community in the most useful way. A range of important considerations began to emerge.

First, we considered that there were a number of adults and children living in the community who were on the fringes of the church. These were people who showed goodwill towards the church by coming to the carol service and to the harvest supper and who supported a stall at the Summer fête, but who neither looked nor felt totally at home in the parish communion or matins on the rare occasions when they came.

We came to appreciate the fact that there exists a considerable cultural barrier between the formal liturgy of the church and the families growing up in a secular society. People who have not been nurtured into the life of the Church of England sit uneasily with so much of the imagery and language which constitutes traditional liturgy. For these fringe members to be integrated into the life of the local church there is an urgent need for some gentle bridge which enables the transition to be made from the secular to the religious culture in a way which is almost unnoticed. Family services need to be able to act as this bridge.

Second, we quickly realised that the Church of England did not have a religious monopoly within the community. Although there were no other chapels or church buildings in the village, some of the people inhabiting the fringes of church life claimed nominal allegiance, if at all, to other Christian traditions. Their memories and expectations of church services may be quite different from those of nominal Anglicans. At the same time, we recognised that there was living within the heart of the community a skilled Methodist local preacher who travelled some distance for his Sunday preaching commitment. We invited him to join our working party and to contribute to a monthly 'united family service'. Joining resources with the resident Methodist local preacher increased the pastoral effectiveness of the enterprise greatly, especially given the fact that both the Anglican priest and reader lived in neighbouring villages.

Third, we needed to listen to the voice of the older or more established Anglicans within the community. The talk of an ecumenical venture gave rise to fears in some that the parish church would be completely departing from a recognised liturgical structure on the third Sunday in the month. My own view was that a united service should neither adopt the theoretically unstructured pattern of the Free Church tradition nor follow directly the liturgical pattern from the Anglican book. We needed to find a compromise position in which the strengths of both Anglicanism and the Free Churches could meet. In practice this meant seeking a specific liturgical structure, but a liturgical structure which would permit a great deal of flexibility.

Fourth, we decided that a monthly family service should try to reflect the life and the potential of the community itself as well as the views of the vicar and of the Methodist local preacher. We wanted to anchor the family service in a house group which existed to take responsibility for the planning. The group was to be as open as possible, specifically inviting some people to certain meetings and hoping and praying that others would come as well.

The task of this planning group was to decide the theme and to plan the content of the monthly service. This meant preparing music, drama and proclamation, as well as choosing hymns and readings. The planning group was free to involve individuals and societies from the village, like the playgroup or the Women's Institute, as appropriate ideas and occasions arose. Again we realised that planning a full fifty minute unstructured service from scratch is incredibly time-consuming and wasteful of resources. Yet another argument seemed to indicate the desirability of finding a regular liturgical pattern which would allow the planning group to assume certain consistencies from month to month, but at the same time give them the opportunity for creative development.

The precedents which we found in neighbouring churches

for a liturgical structure to a family service were of two main kinds. Some followed a pattern derived from matins, making use of an opening bidding, versicles, responses and perhaps the Venite. Others relied heavily on the creation of new material. Neither route seemed entirely satisfactory for our own situation. The problem with both models is that they fail to lead into the mainstream life of the worshipping community.

The danger in creating a form of family service which is so dissimilar from what the local church is doing in its other services is that the family service tends to build up a congregation of its own which remains isolated from the rest of the local church. The family service congregation still feels out of place at other church services, even if they are held in the same building! In other words, if one of the major aims of the family service is to build a bridge between the unchurched and the life of the local church, we must make sure that this bridge actually leads somewhere and does not merely become an end in itself.

Structure

These considerations led us to design a family service made up entirely from the components of the eucharist which the church would be using on the other Sundays in the month. The service which we designed included four main sections. The first section, preparation, followed a formal pattern. The second section, ministry of the word, allowed complete freedom. The third section, prayers, combined the opportunity for creative freedom with a liturgical structure. The fourth section, conclusion, like the opening section, followed a formal pattern.

In designing this form of service we deliberately did not write into the structure fixed places for hymns. We envisaged that often we would want an opening hymn before the preparation, two or three hymns somewhere in the ministry of the word and a closing hymn between the prayers and the conclusion. We felt it important, however, to allow the specific theme chosen for individual services to determine the points within the liturgical framework where hymns would be most appropriate.

Generally our family services open with an informal word of welcome, the announcement of the theme for the day and an opening hymn. Then the first section of the service, the preparation, follows this fixed pattern:

Greeting: We begin the family service with the greeting 'The Lord be with you', in exactly the same way as we begin the parish communion.

Opening prayer (collect for purity): The opening prayer also follows the pattern of the parish communion as a preparation for worship.

Collect: The collect for the day, or a special prayer chosen to reflect the theme of the service, follows on immediately from the collect for purity. The collect is placed in this early position, well in advance of the ministry of the word, to demonstrate how the theme of the day has a vital part in the formal liturgical structure of the opening.

Prayers of penitence: The kyrie and confession examine our relationship with God early on in the service. The words of absolution celebrate the forgiveness which enables us to approach God in confidence.

Peace: The peace follows on immediately from the confession and absolution, demonstrating that the restoration of right relationship with God is also reflected in right relationships one with another. The peace gives the congregation the opportunity to greet one another and to relax in greater informality.

The second part of the service, the ministry of the word, is totally unstructured and left to the ministers or planning group to design differently for each occasion. As a rule, the ministry of the word includes hymns, one or two passages from scripture and a variety of other material, but the order in which these come depends on the total structure of what the planning group intends to include in the service.

The third section of the family service, the prayers, again follows a formal pattern from the eucharist. This section is made up of two parts:

Prayer of intercessions and thanksgivings: The prayer of intercessions and thanksgivings allows us to follow a fixed pattern of praying for the church, for the world, for our community, for the sick and suffering and for the departed. At the same time this pattern of prayer allows plenty of freedom for the development of specific intentions suggested by the overall theme of each family service.

Lord's prayer: We conclude the prayers by joining together in the Christian family prayer.

The prayers tend to lead into the final hymn, usually chosen to tie in with the theme of the day. Then the final part of the family service, the conclusion, contains two components:

Praise: We want to end the family service on a note of praise and choose for this purpose the ancient canticle 'Glory to God in the highest'. This is the climax towards which the direction of the family service moves.

Blessing and dismissal: The service ends, as it begins, in exactly the same way as the parish communion, with the blessing and dismissal.

In selecting these particular components from the eucharist to form the structure of our liturgical family service, we were careful not to assume too much of the congregation. We invite the congregation to share in the confession, the peace, the prayer of intercessions and thanksgivings and the Lord's prayer. We do not, however, include the creed in our regular form of family service on the grounds that not everyone present can be assumed to want to identify with such a sharp statement of faith. On occasions when the theme of the service gives special point to a profession of faith, the creed can always be included in the context of the ministry of the word and to follow on naturally from specific teaching. We were also careful to choose the words of the peace not to assume that the congregation only included those who could say 'we were all baptised into one body'. Part of our hope was that the unbaptised would be present at this form of service as well!

Having agreed this form of service, we recognised that we needed to produce appropriate material for use in the pews. On the one hand, we realised that the hymns and other material specific to the theme of the day would need to be printed out specially for each service. On the other hand, we wanted the continuity of the liturgical framework from month to month to be very apparent. Our solution was to produce an order of service booklet which would contain all the basic material used each time and in the clearest and most accessible manner possible. We wanted to make the service booklet attractive for young children as well as for their parents, and so designed it to include a set of simple illustrations.

Our final consideration was to find a name for this form of service which we had created. Our working title had been 'family worship'; but the more we thought about the title, the more uneasy we became. The emphasis on family services in today's church seems to ignore the large part of the worshipping community and of the potential worshipping community who are not members of a conventional family structure. After considerable reflection we decided to call our order of service simply *Come and Worship!*

Practice

The service booklet *Come and Worship!* was used as the regular structure for the monthly family service. Experience of using this form of service suggests that it adequately meets the needs we had identified. On the one hand, those familiar with the liturgical structure of Anglican worship found the framework sufficient to anchor their participation in the monthly family service. On the other hand, the Methodist local preacher, coming from an entirely different tradition, did not feel himself hidebound by the structure. The planning group found that they had lots of decisions to make and material to prepare for the ministry of the word, without being overwhelmed by having to structure from scratch a full fifty minute service each month. Children and adults on the fringes of church life felt able to participate easily in the monthly family service, without being expected either to know much about the regular liturgical structure of Anglican worship or to assent to too many implicit or explicit religious assumptions. Moreover, they also discovered that when they came to a parish communion service, on one of the other Sundays in the month or at the major Christian festivals, they were already familiar with much of the service.

During a typical month the *Come and Worship!* service would actively involve quite a large number of people from the community, not only in preparation beforehand but also in leading the service itself. A lay person who had taken a particular responsibility in structuring the theme for the day might well come forward from his or her seat to welcome the congregation, announce the theme and lead into the opening hymn. Another lay person might lead the formal opening of the service.

Next, the ministry of the word could involve a range of skills from the local community. The theme of the day might include a short piece of drama worked out by three or four adults. Children might have been invited beforehand to prepare a song or to offer a picture or a model. The planning group might have decided to include a passage from scripture or from a novel to be read by a range of voices spread out around the church building. Sometimes pre-recorded music might be played or a sequence of pictures or slides used. Sometimes the prayer of intercessions and thanksgivings might be divided up among five voices, each preparing a short bidding for the distinct sections of the prayer. On some occasions the Methodist local preacher or I would decide that we wanted to include a more traditional teaching ministry, involving a short sermon, exhortation or meditation.

More and more I discovered that I was able to watch the service run itself. Sometimes I found myself sitting in the congregation instead of at the vicar's prayer desk, or accepting an invitation to lead a service in another parish, while the laity took charge of the family service without my supervision or intervention.

Note

The form of family service developed for this parish was subsequently published by Mowbray as the service booklet *Come and Worship!*

Contributors

Mrs Gill Ambrose is Religious Education Adviser in Children's Work for the Diocese of Ely.

The Revd Stephen Cottrell is the Diocesan Missioner and Bishop's Chaplain for Evangelism in the Diocese of Wakefield.

Mrs Margaret Dean is Diocesan Children's Education Officer for the Diocese of Guildford.

Mrs Anne Faulkner is Parish Development Adviser for the Buckinghamshire Archdeaconry in the Diocese of Oxford.

The Revd Professor Leslie J Francis is D J James Professor of Pastoral Theology at Trinity College Carmarthen and University of Wales Lampeter.

The Revd Betty Pedley is Parish Education Advisor (Children) and Bishop's Chaplain for Children for the Diocese of Wakefield.

Mrs Marion Richards is Provincial Adviser for Children's Ministry for the Church in Wales.

Mr Michael Sturdy is a member of the education committee at All Saints', Wokingham, in the Diocese of Oxford.

Mrs Anne Thorne was formerly Sunday School Leader of St James', Exeter, in the Diocese of Exeter, and is now an ordinand in training.

The Revd Prebendary Brian R Tubbs is Vicar of St John the Baptist, Paignton, in the Diocese of Exeter.

The Revd Martin Warner is Administrator of the Shrine of Our Lady of Walsingham in the Diocese of Norwich.

Mrs Angela Warwick was formerly churchwarden of St Mary's, Datchet, in the Diocese of Oxford.